Enchanted Realms

A Guided Drawing Journey

AN INTERACTIVE SKETCHBOOK TO CREATE CHARACTERS, CREATURES, AND PLACES OF DARK ROMANCE

Walter Foster

With 50+ prompts and art to spark your creativity

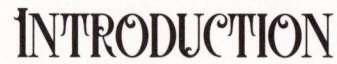

INTRODUCTION
Drawing Enchanted Realms

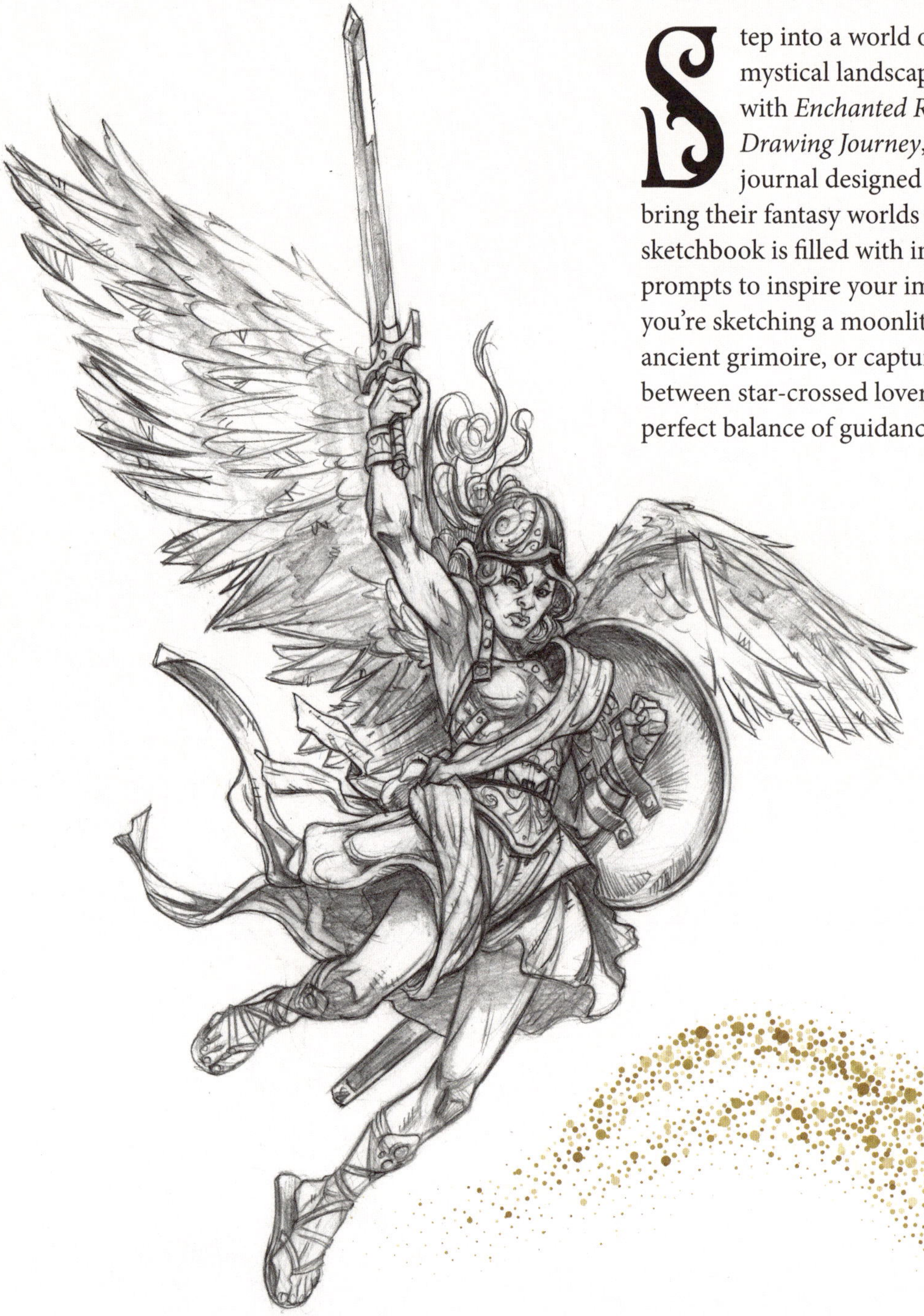

Step into a world of enchanted castles, mystical landscapes, and magical creatures with *Enchanted Realms—A Guided Drawing Journey,* a one-of-a-kind creative journal designed for those who want to bring their fantasy worlds to life. This spellbinding sketchbook is filled with inspiring art and guided prompts to inspire your imagination. Whether you're sketching a moonlit fae court, designing an ancient grimoire, or capturing a romantic moment between star-crossed lovers, this book offers the perfect balance of guidance and creative freedom.

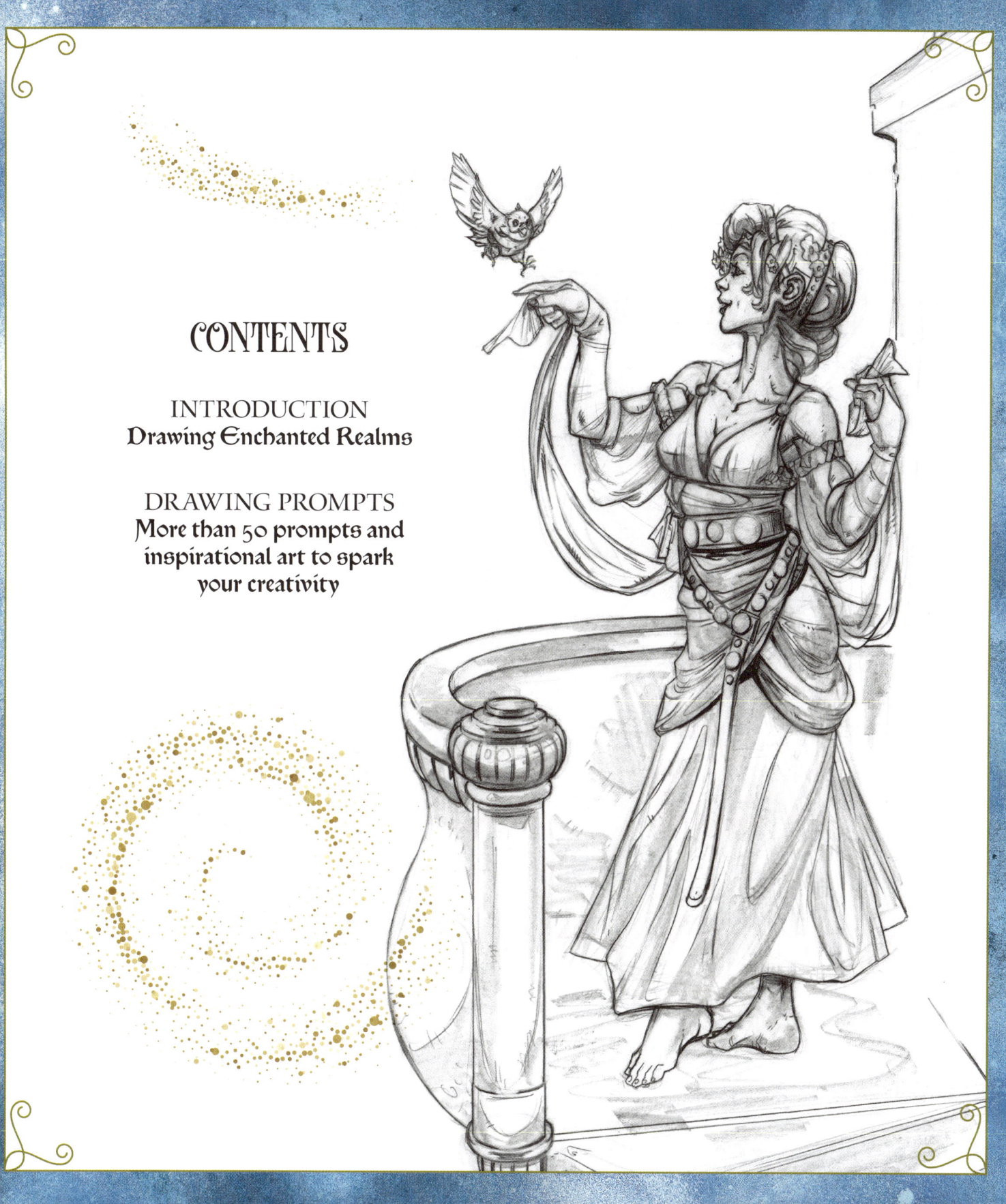

CONTENTS

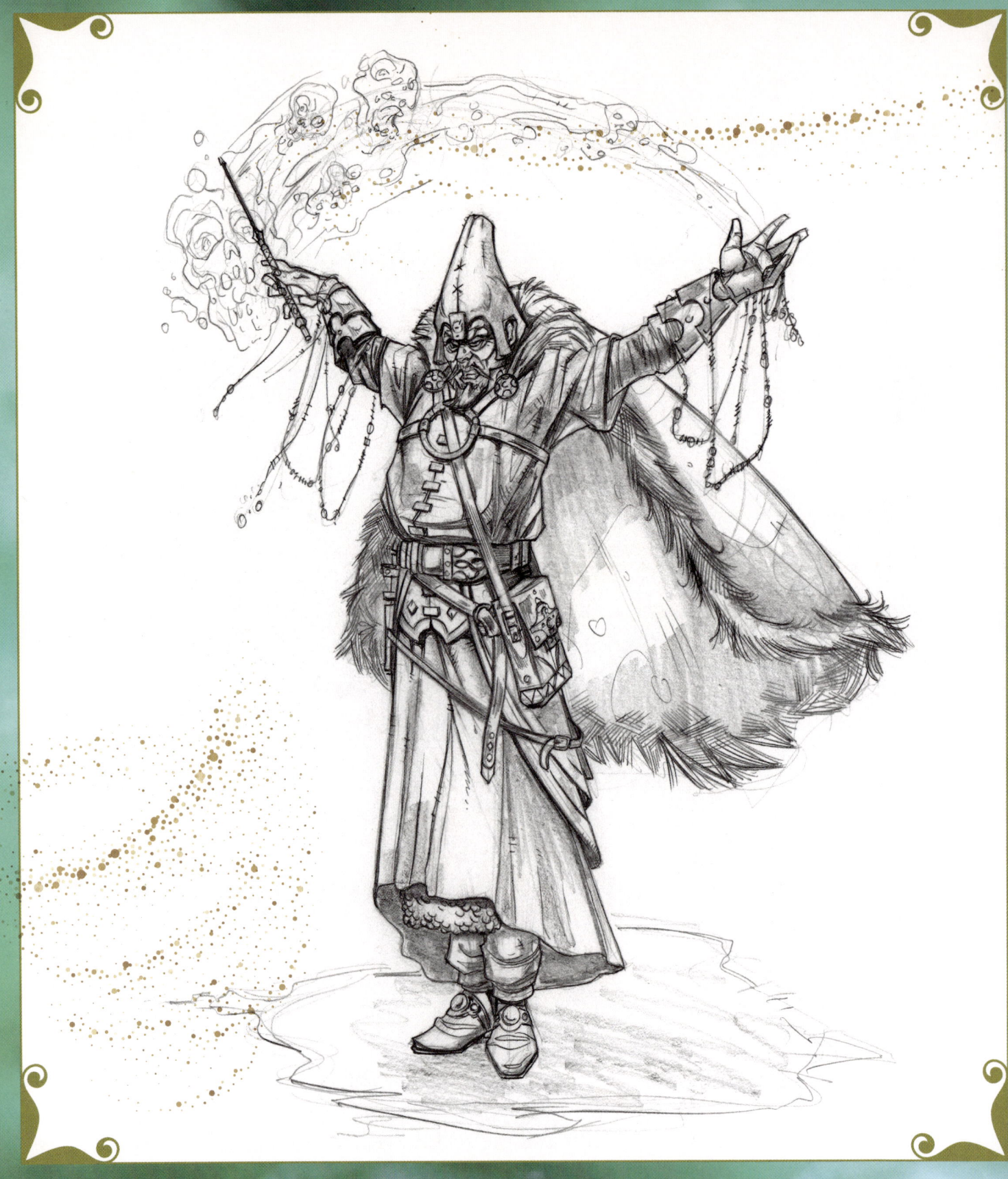

Conjure a sorcerer mid-incantation, his curse spiraling
into the night like smoke made of shadows.

Wander into a charmed forest path where the trees lean close as if whispering ancient secrets.

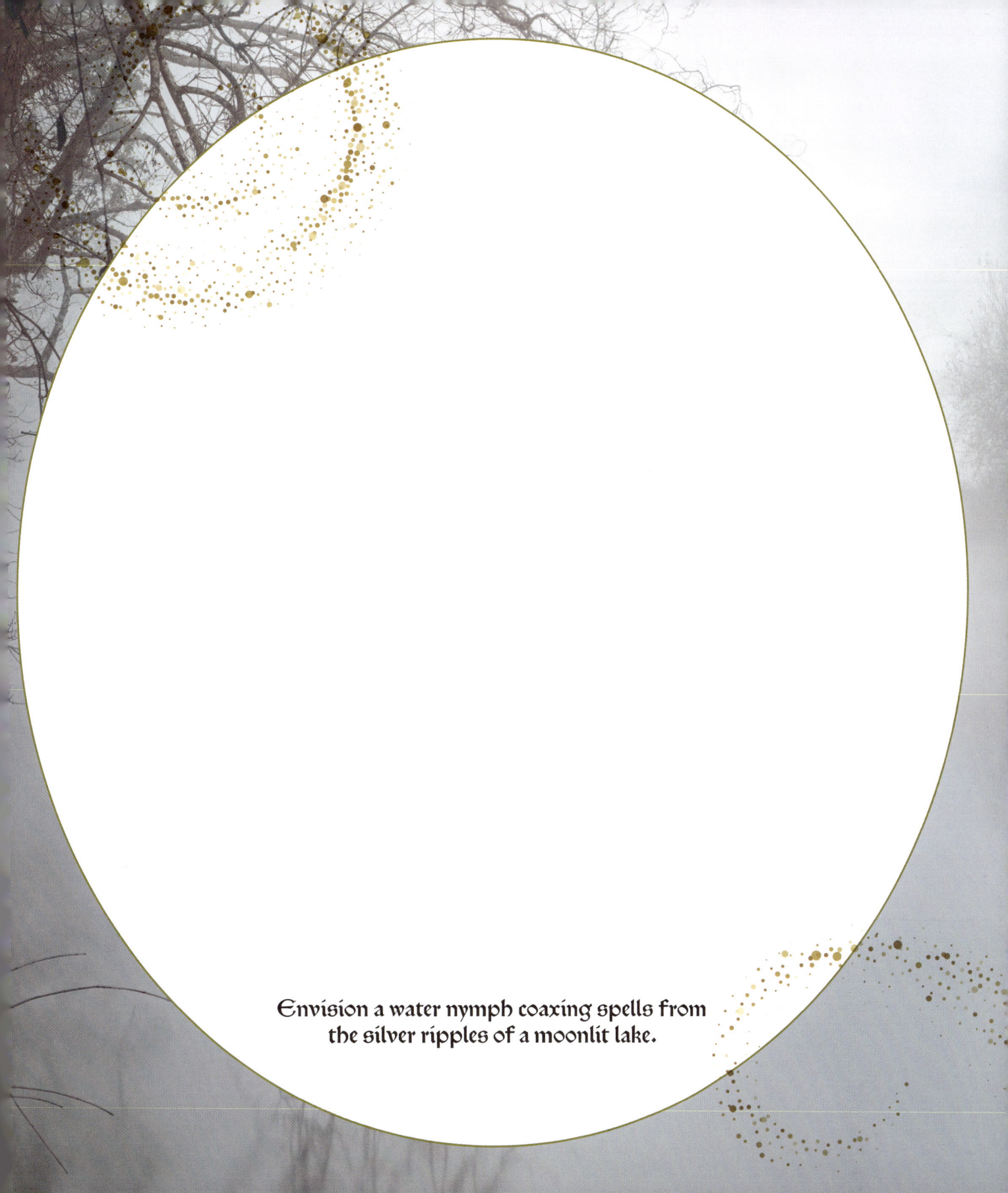

Envision a water nymph coaxing spells from
the silver ripples of a moonlit lake.

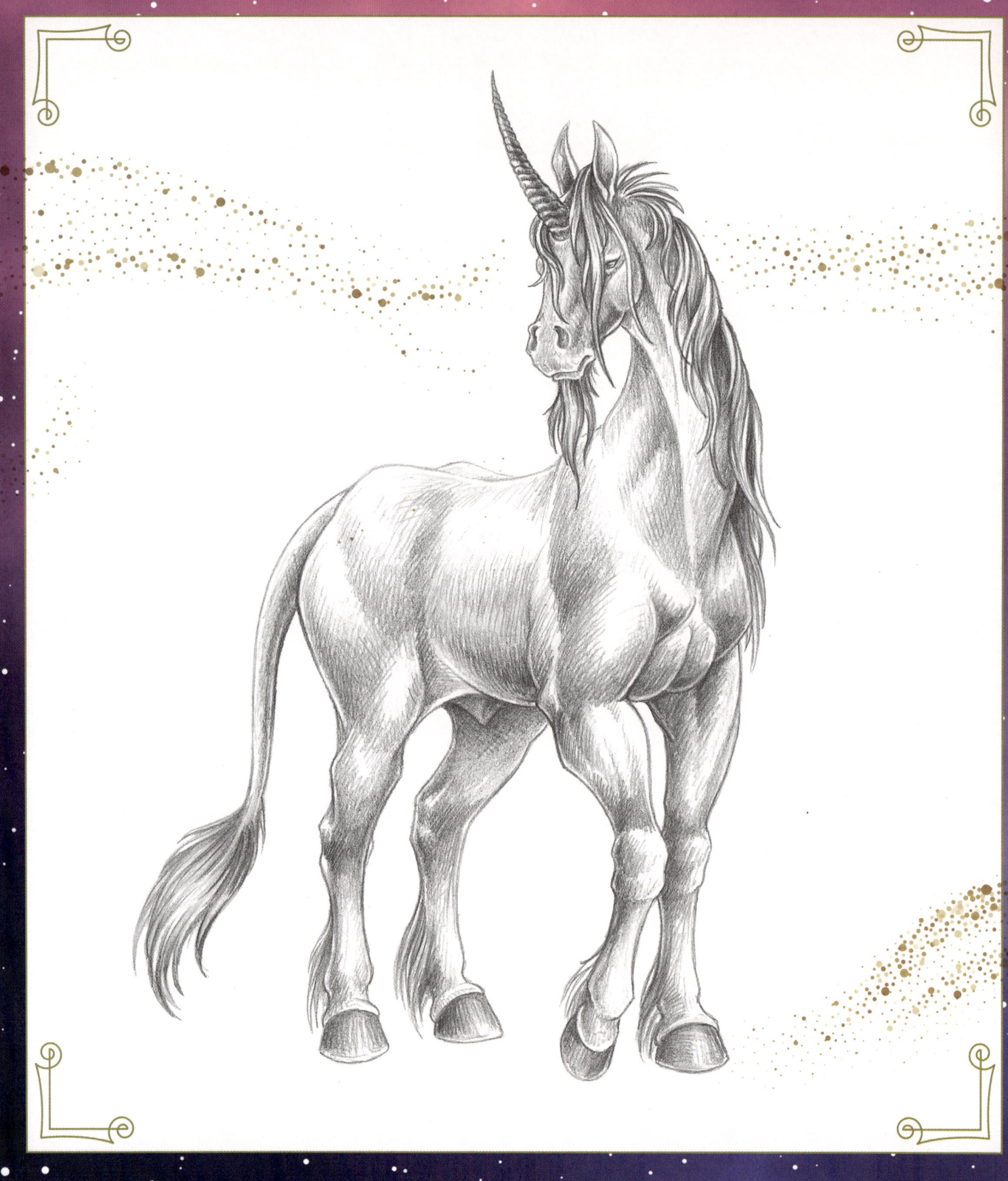

Draw a unicorn with a spiraling horn and a cascading mane.

Create a mountain range so tall its jagged peaks, crowned with glittering celestial temples, pierce the heavens.

Imagine an ornate sword, its blade
shimmering with otherworldly light
and etched with forgotten runes.

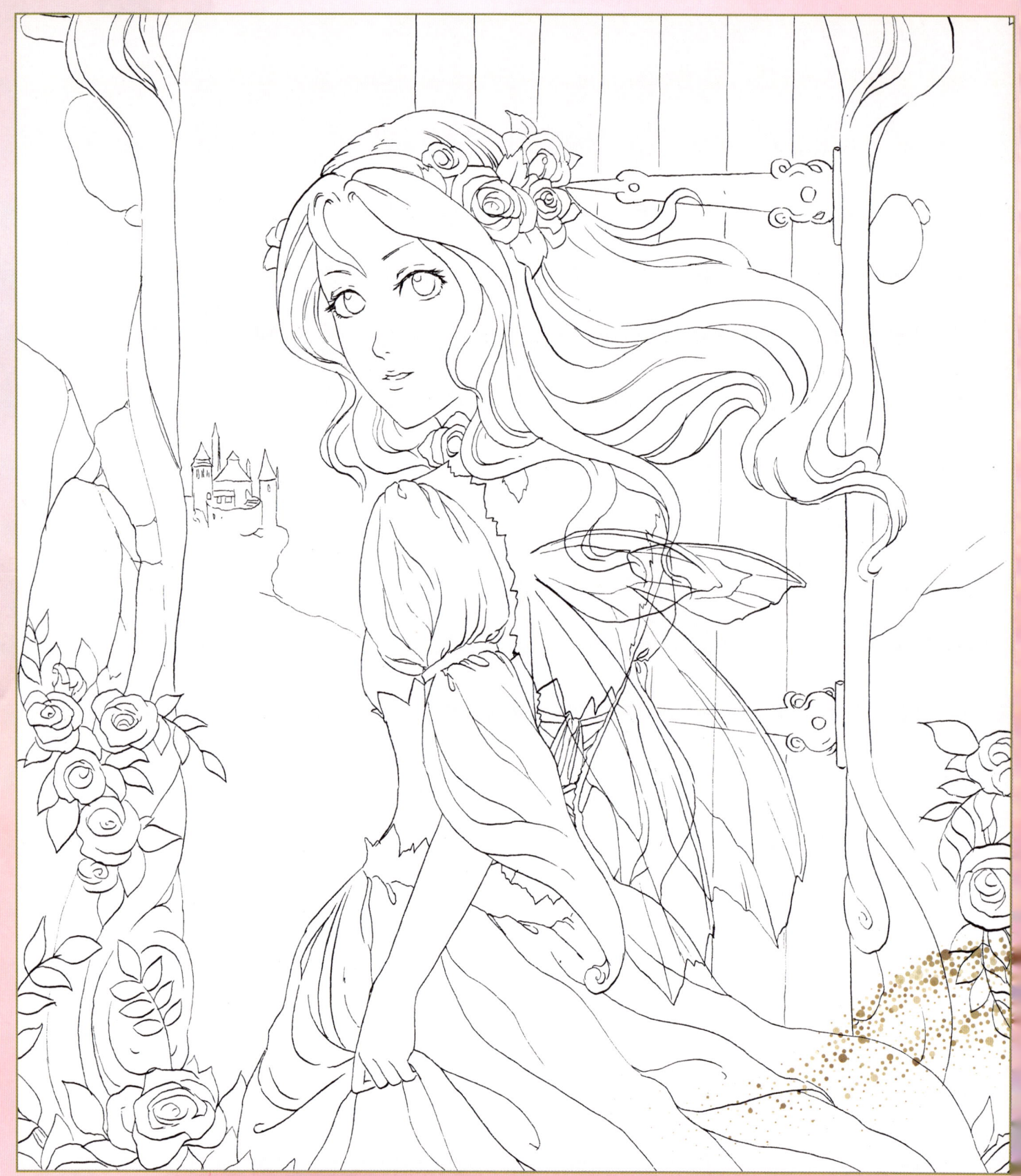

Reveal a fae princess wandering through her enchanted garden, blossoms lining her path.

Sketch an ancient library filled with spellbound tomes that float from shelf to shelf.

Depict a circle of figures
beneath a full moon, casting a
luminous spell by moonlight.

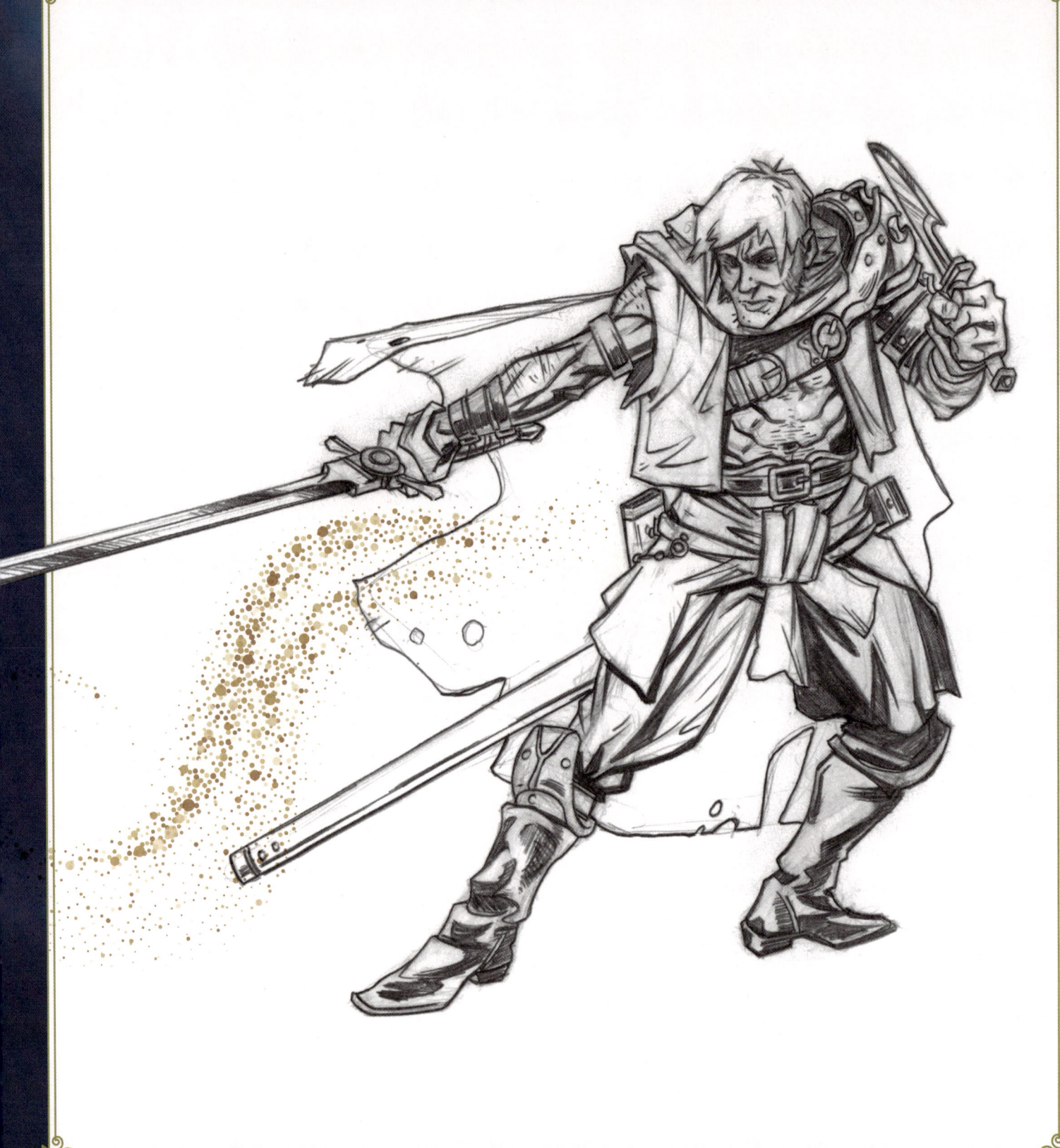

Envision a battle-worn swordsman braced for battle,
blades gleaming in either hand.

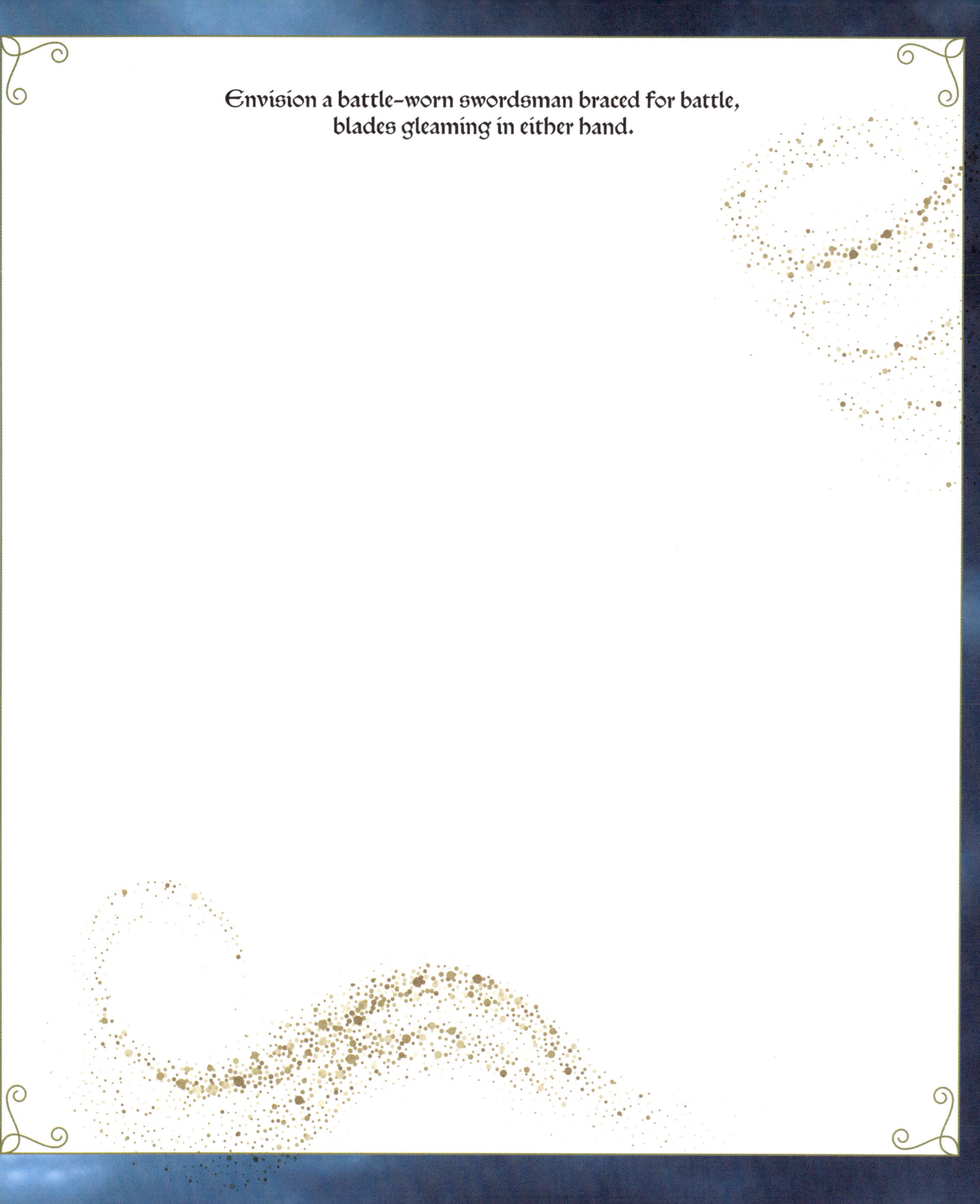

Imagine a cursed mirror that reveals
what the beholder fears they might become.

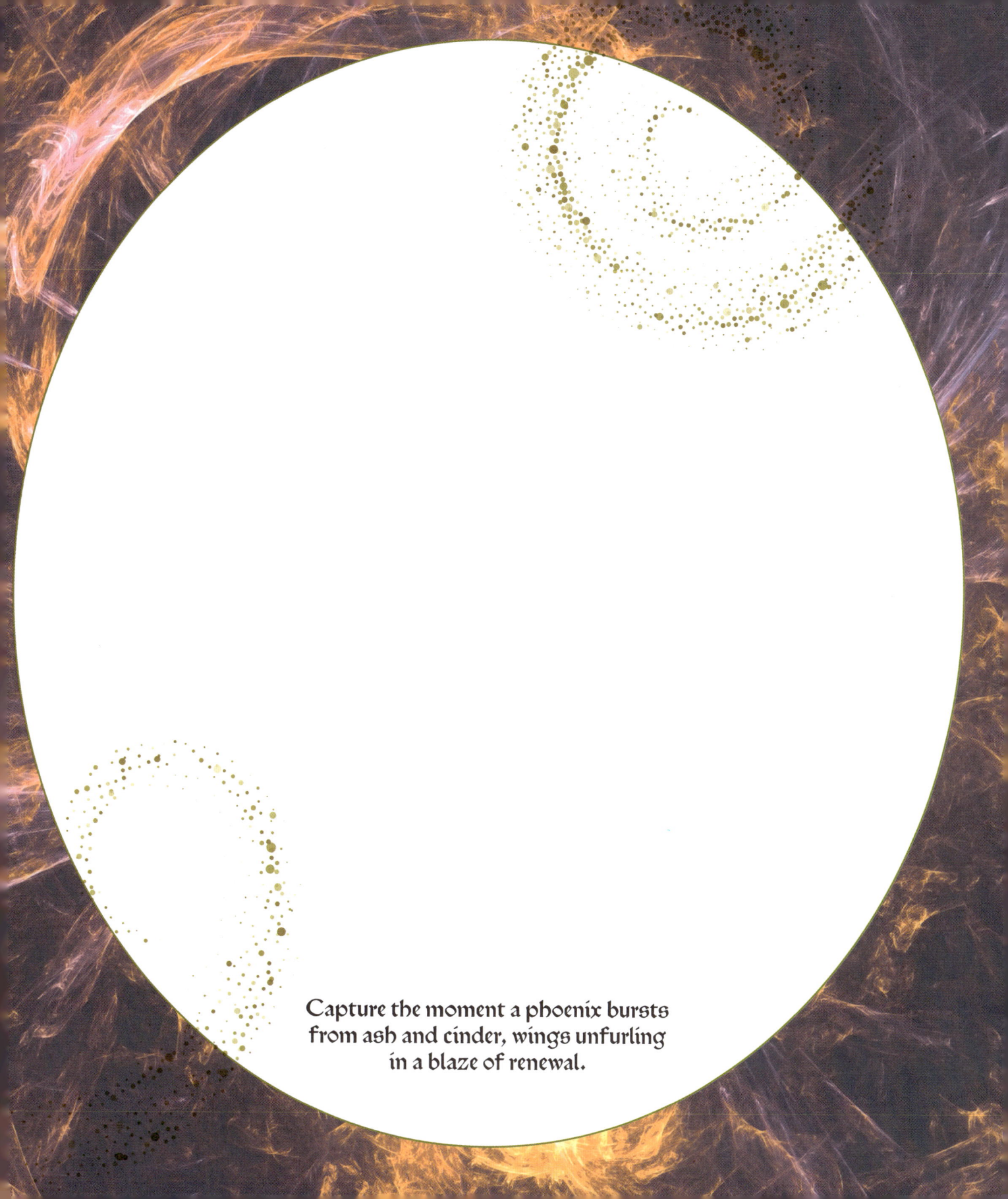

Capture the moment a phoenix bursts
from ash and cinder, wings unfurling
in a blaze of renewal.

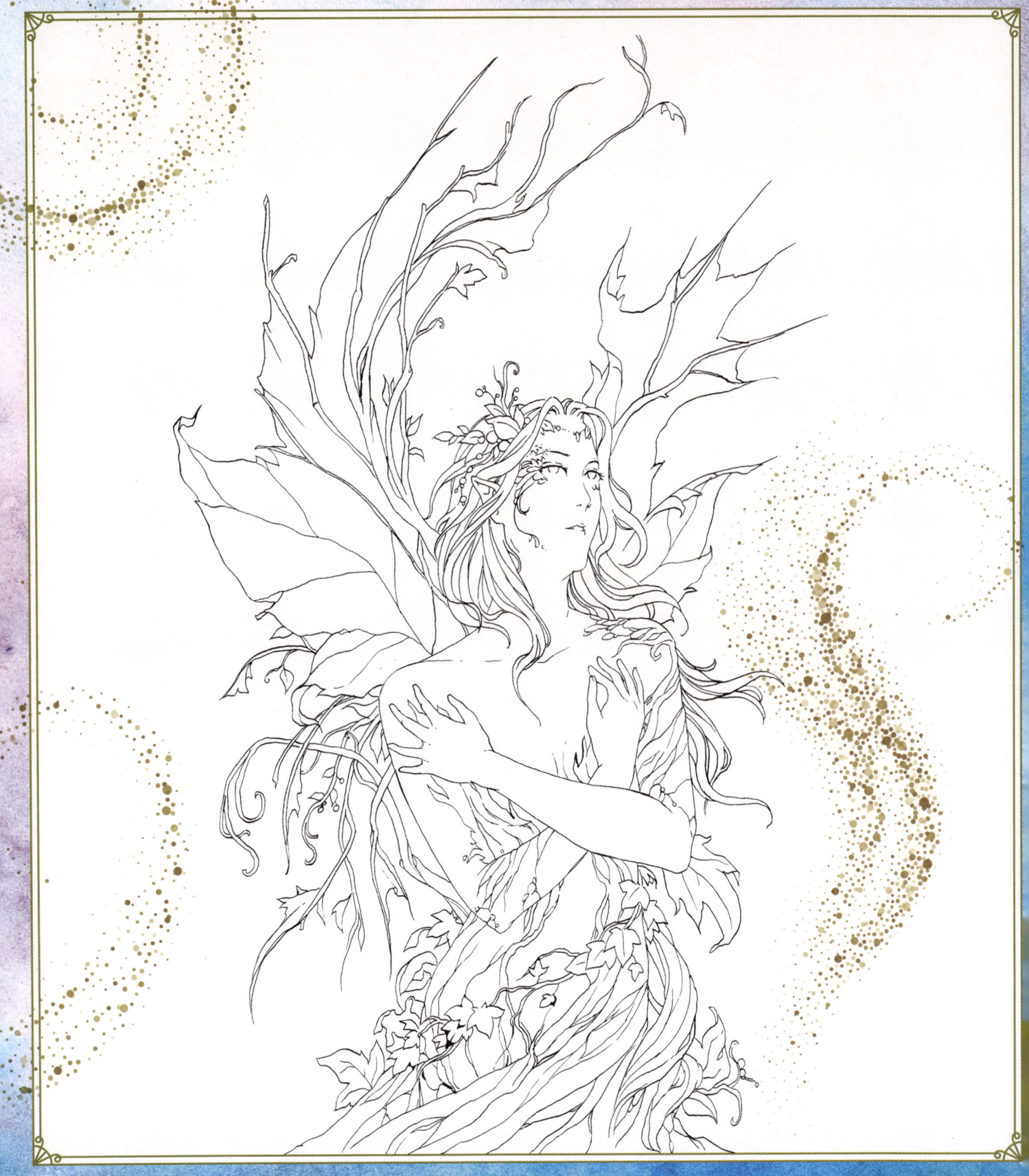

Sketch a forest fae with wings like leaves unfurled,
gazing skyward in quiet wonder.

Portray a mystic river
glowing with enchanted light
as it winds through the dark.

Imagine a masquerade where magic shimmers in the air.

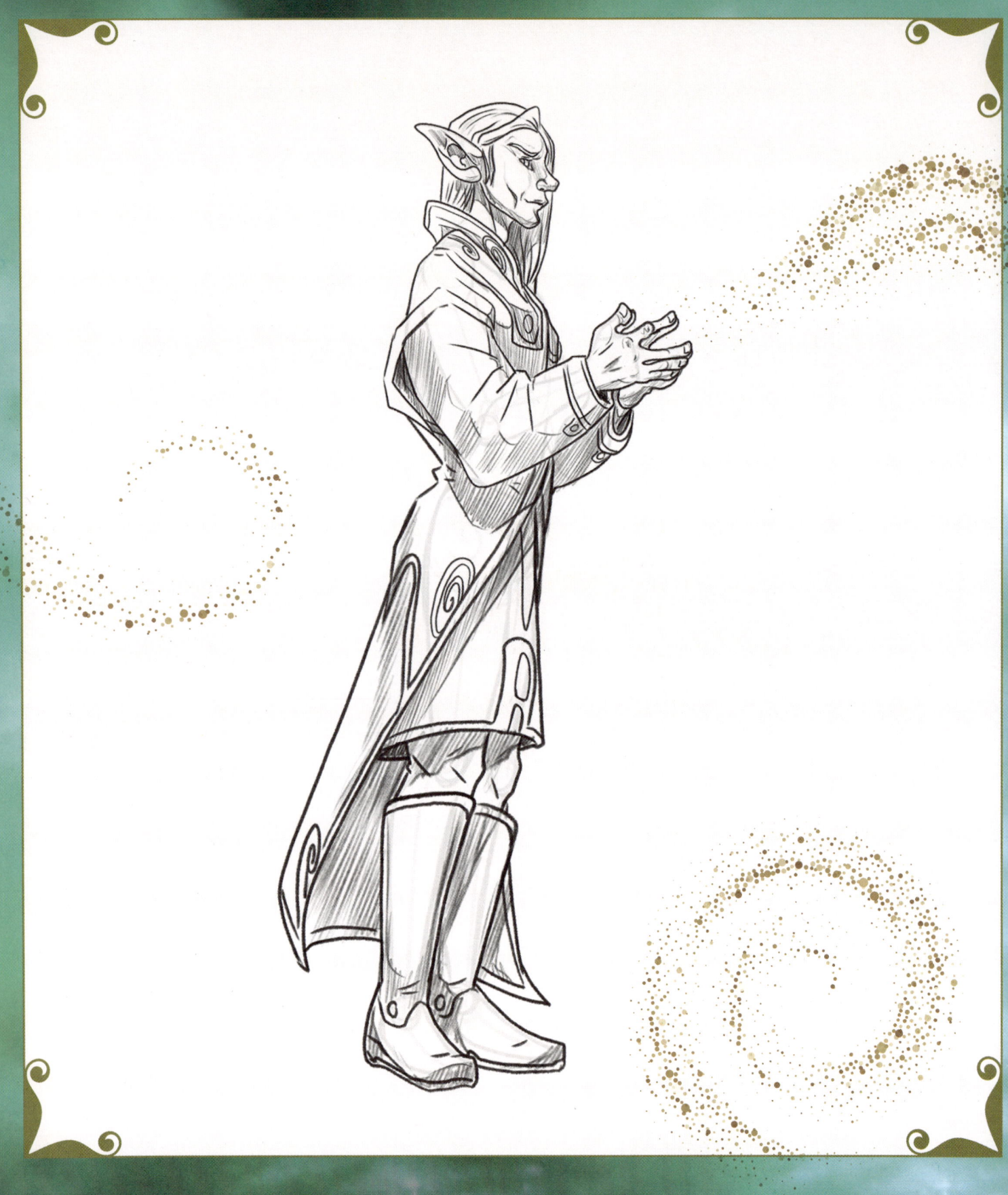

Sketch an elf in elegant robes, hands clasped as though
in quiet thought or spellcraft.

Draw ancient ruins with crumbling
arches cloaked in winding ivy.

Envision planets aligned in a radiant night sky, with moons and stars forming a perfect sigil that casts an otherworldly glow across the land below.

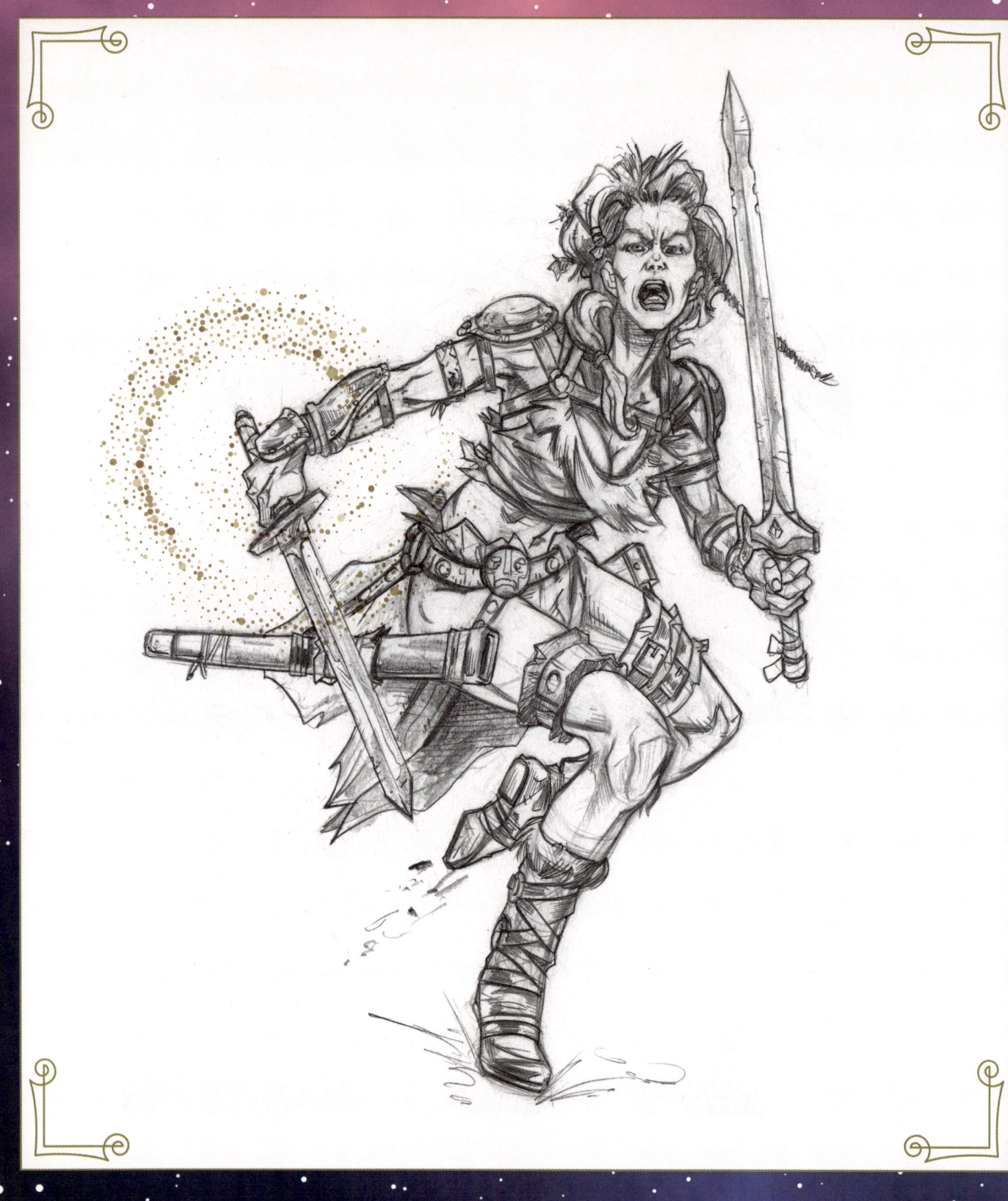

Capture a woman warrior mid-charge,
sword lifted high and eyes blazing.

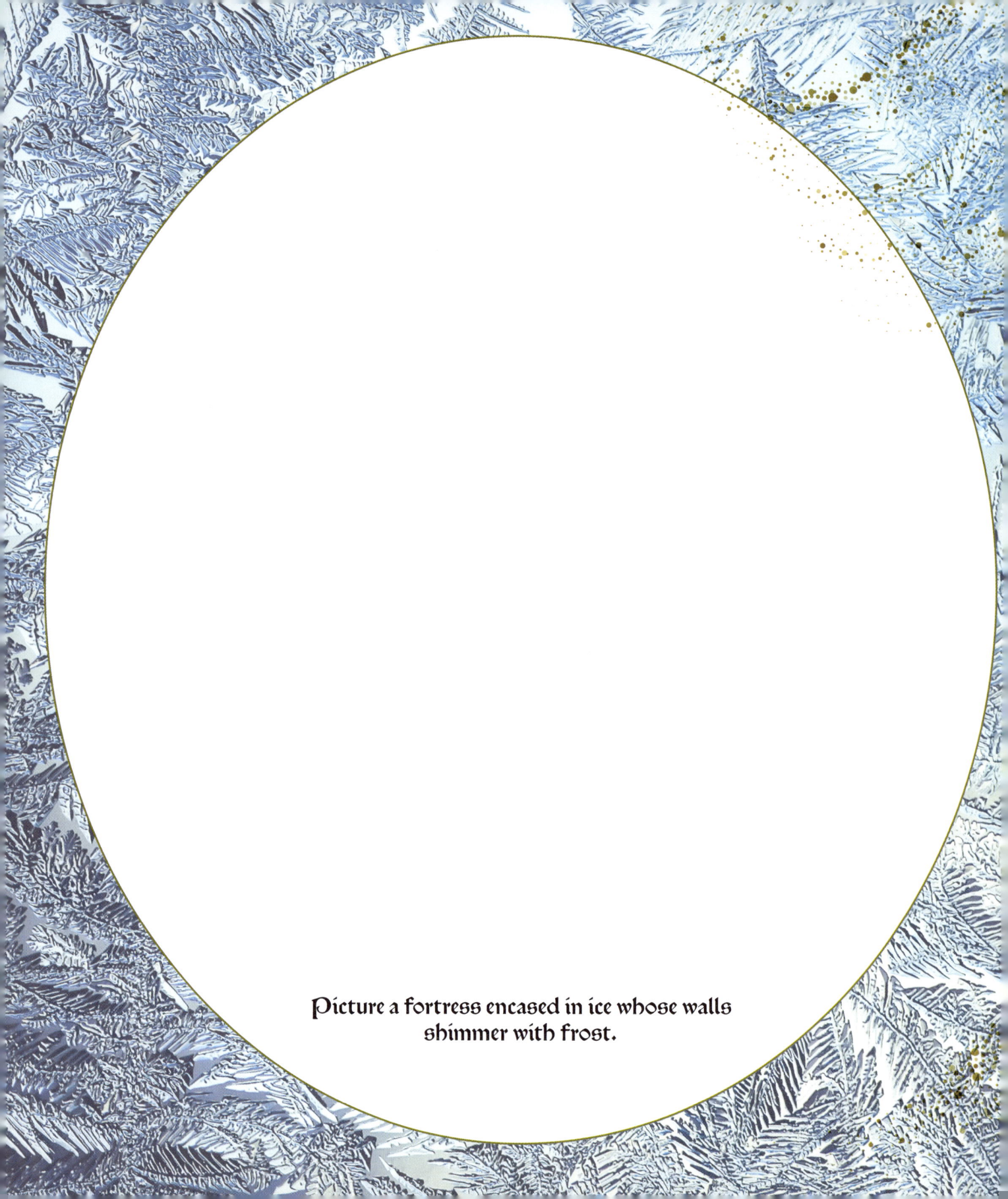

Picture a fortress encased in ice whose walls
shimmer with frost.

Imagine an enchanted fountain whose waters scatter droplets that transform into fleeting visions.

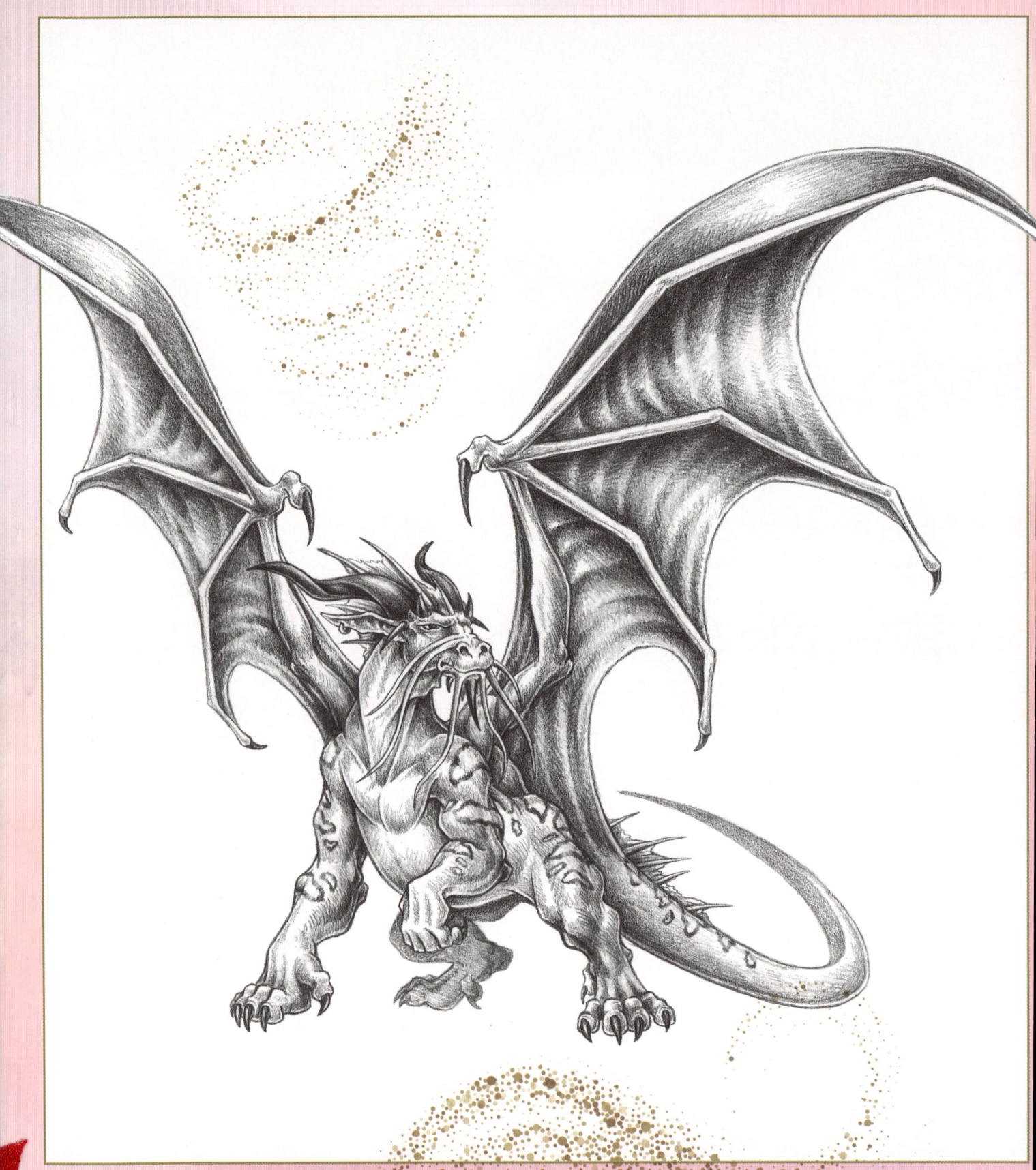

Sketch a dragon with wings outstretched, fangs bared as it crouches to strike.

Depict a crimson moon rising over
shadowed hills, casting its eerie light
across the land, awakening forgotten
curses and summoning restless spirits.

Imagine a cavern filled with luminous crystals where stalactites blaze with light and the air itself vibrates with hidden energy.

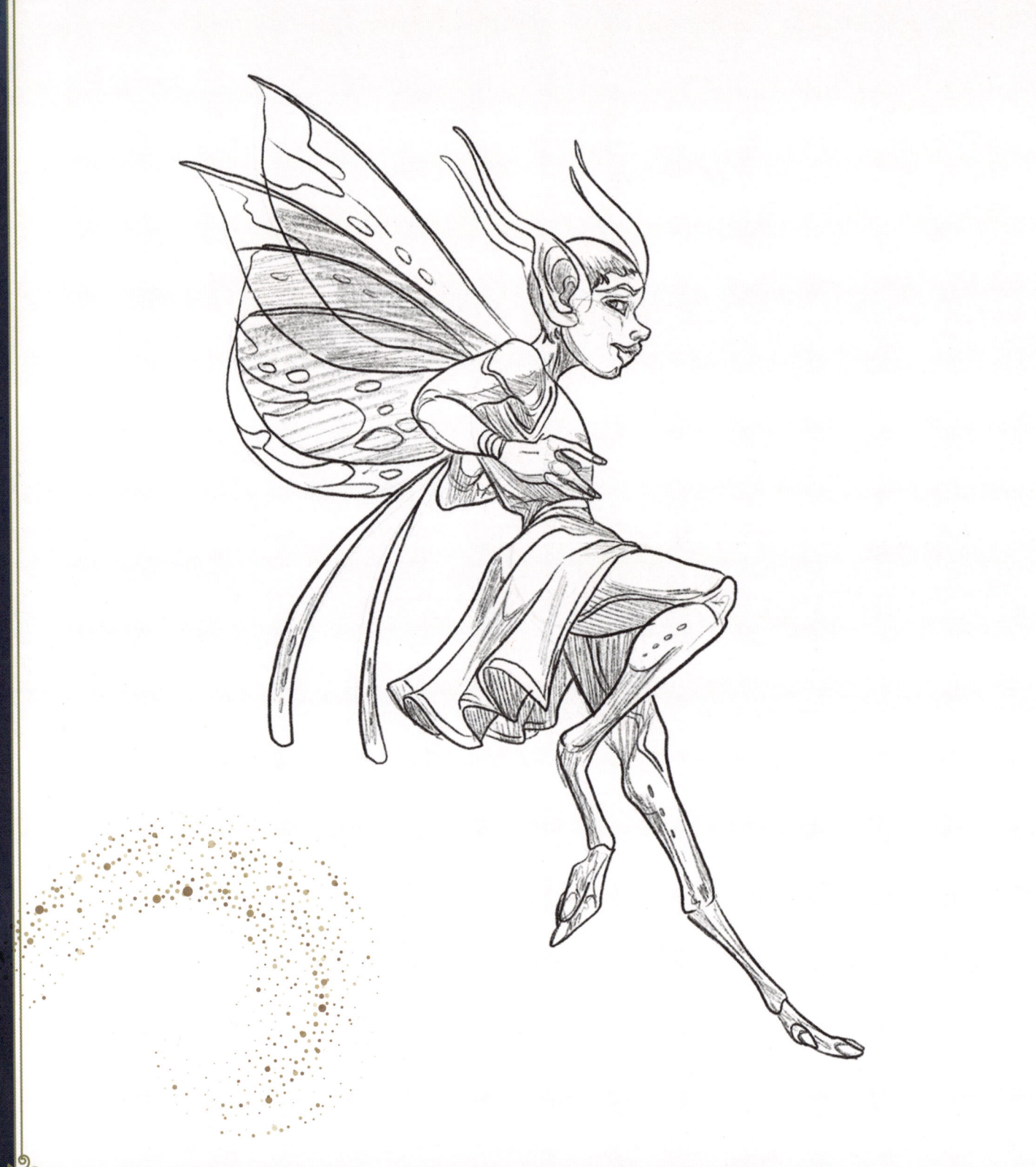

Draw a mischievous fae girl darting through the air,
her gossamer wings shimmering with delicate patterns.

Conjure a throne woven from living vines, its crown of roses blooming as its thorns pierce the stone beneath.

Envision an abandoned cathedral, dust swirling
in colored shafts filtered through stained glass.

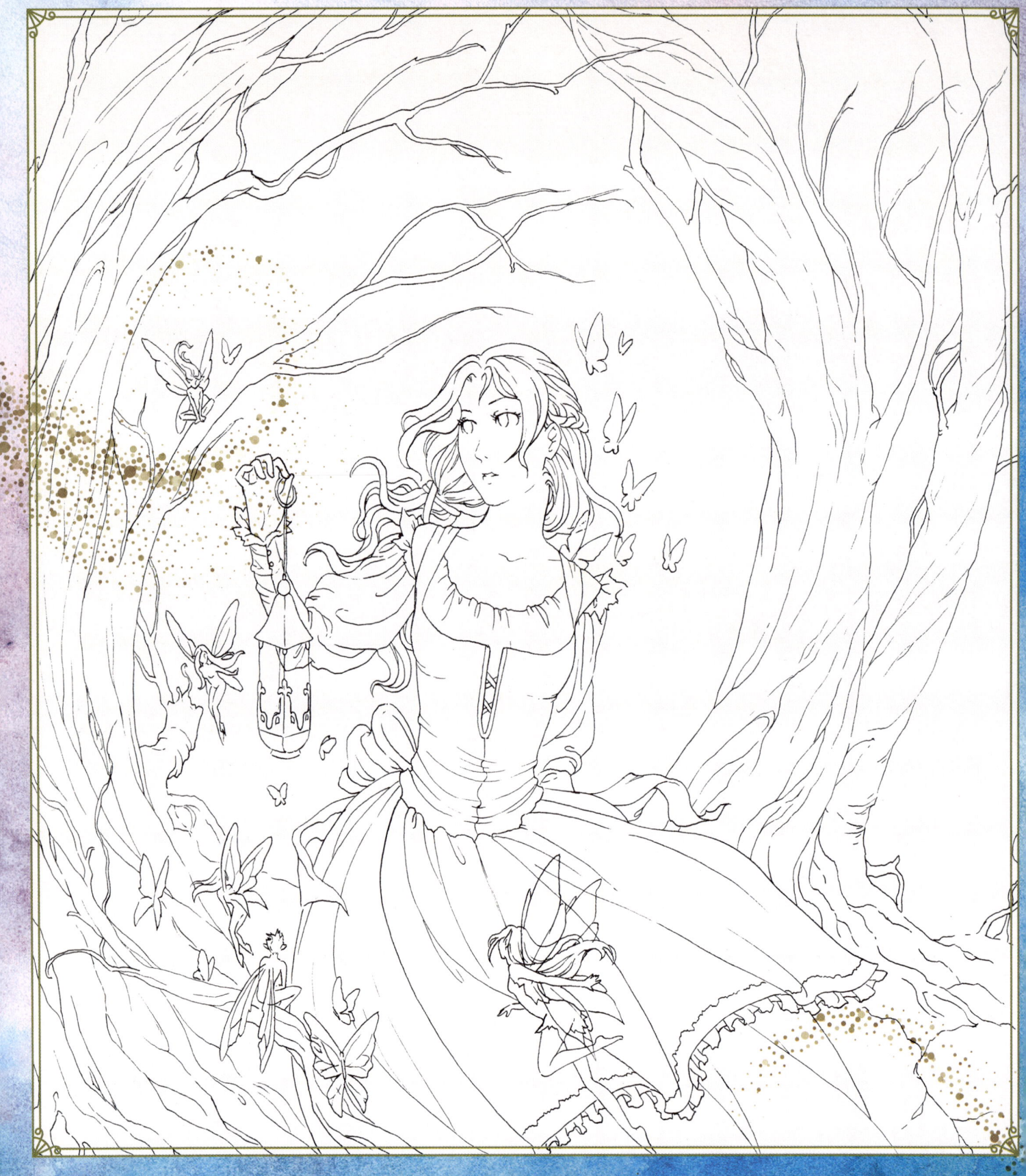

Reveal a maiden holding a lantern, standing within
a ring of trees alive with fluttering fae.

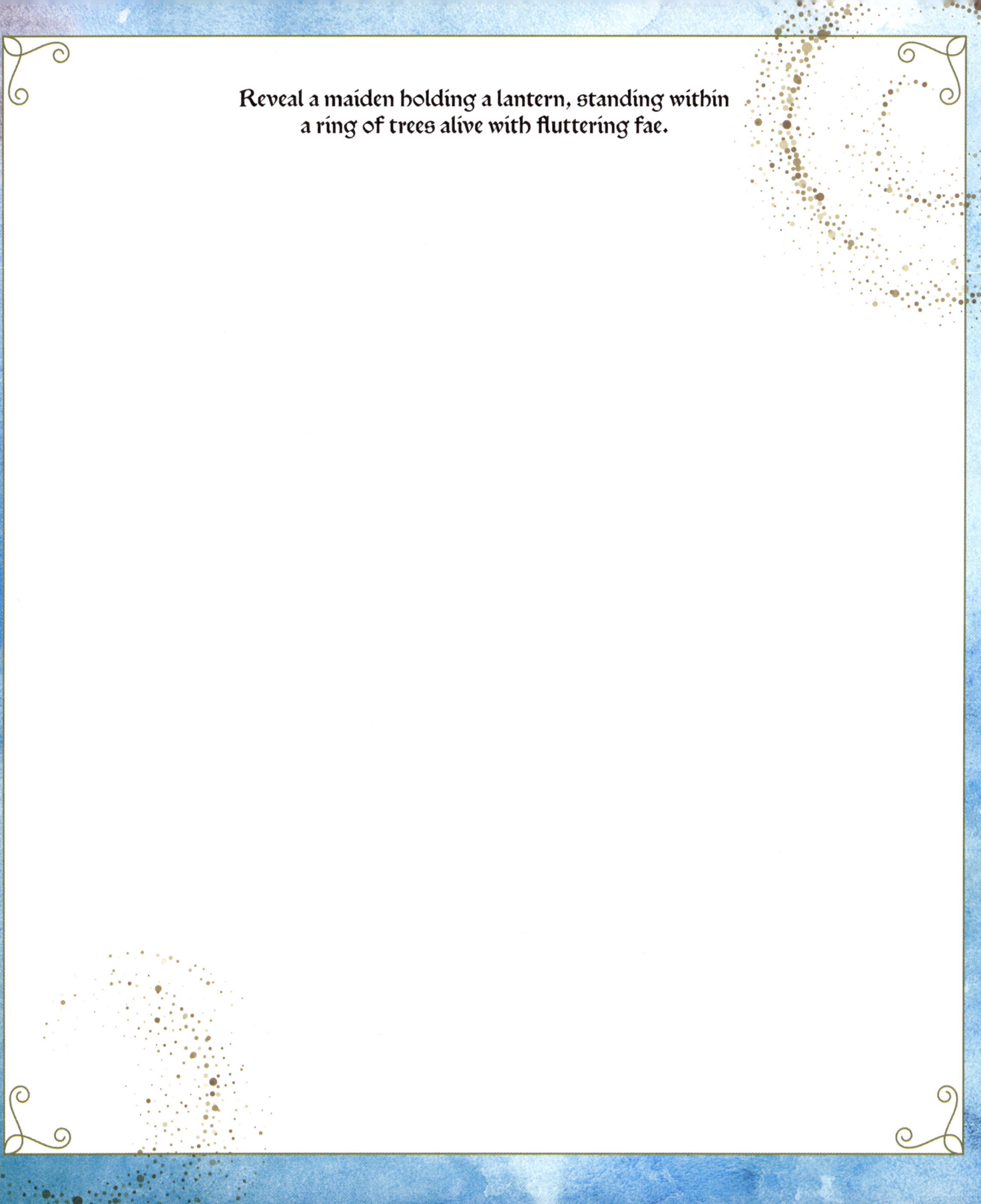

Imagine a haunted battlefield, armor and banners scattered across the earth as ghostly warriors fight an endless war.

Capture an oracle gazing into a glowing
pool where shifting visions show both
the past and futures yet to come.

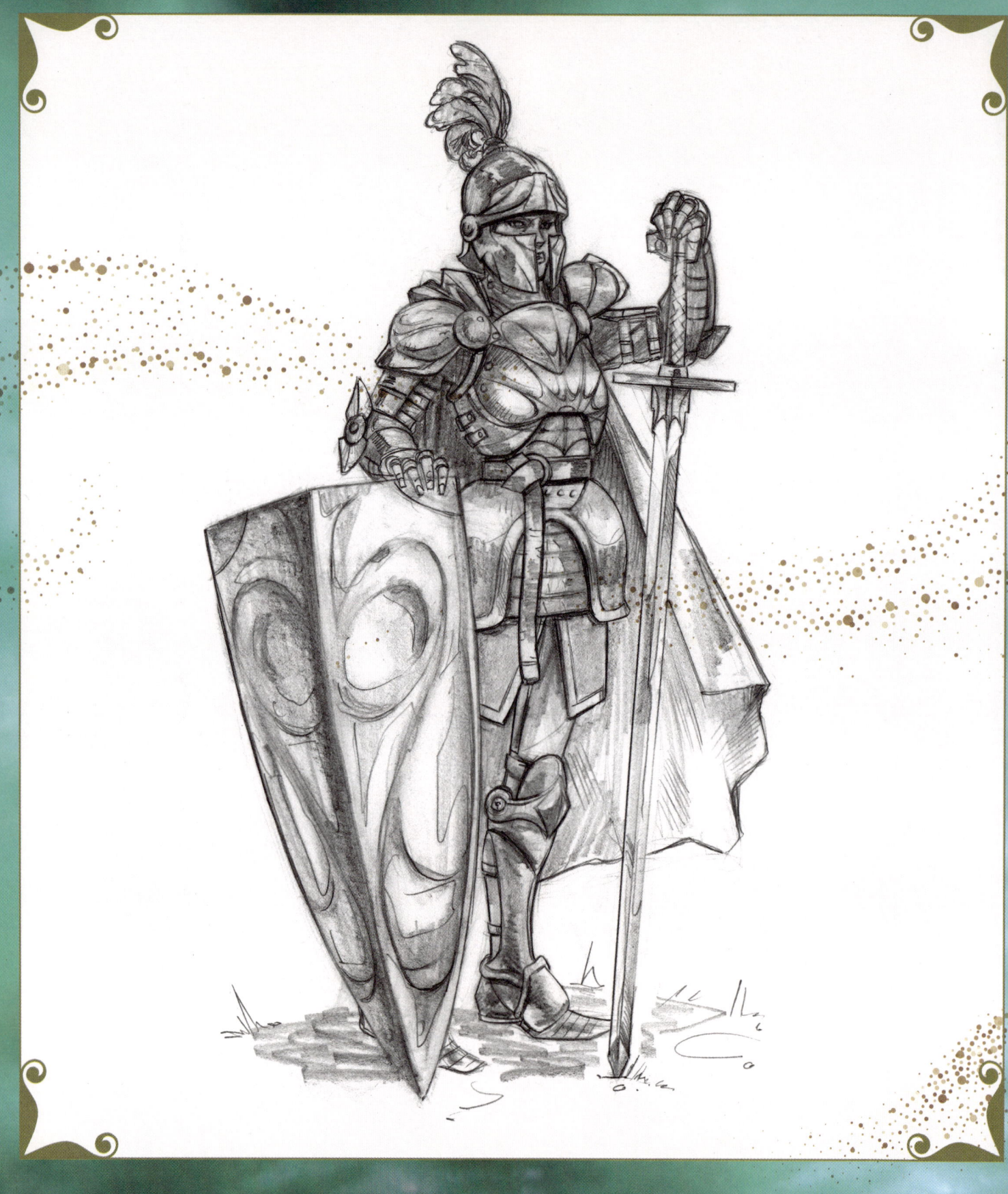

Summon a black knight, armored and unyielding, shield and sword at the ready.

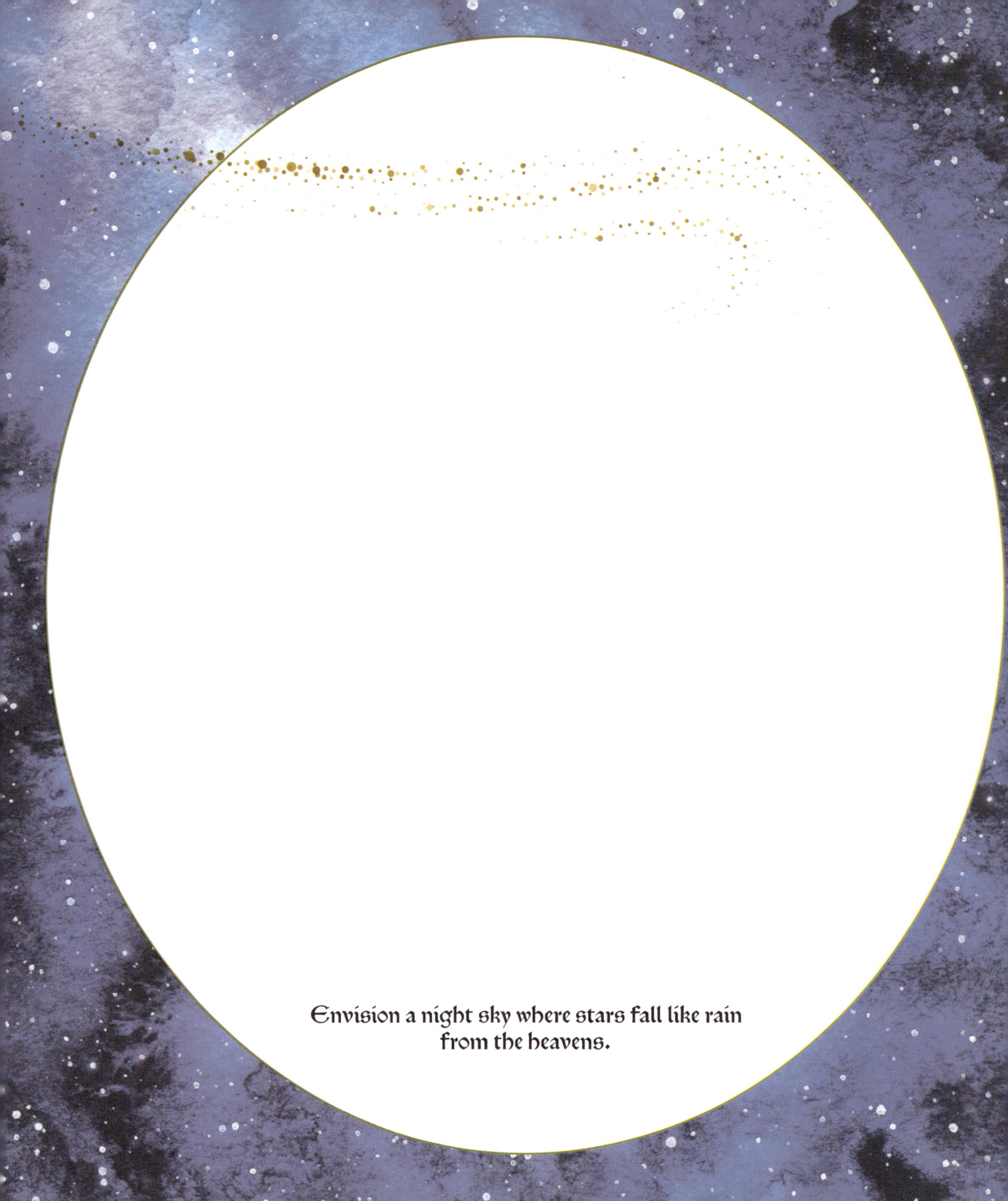

Envision a night sky where stars fall like rain
from the heavens.

Imagine a colossal tree with a carved door at its roots,
its branches rising high enough to scrape the clouds.

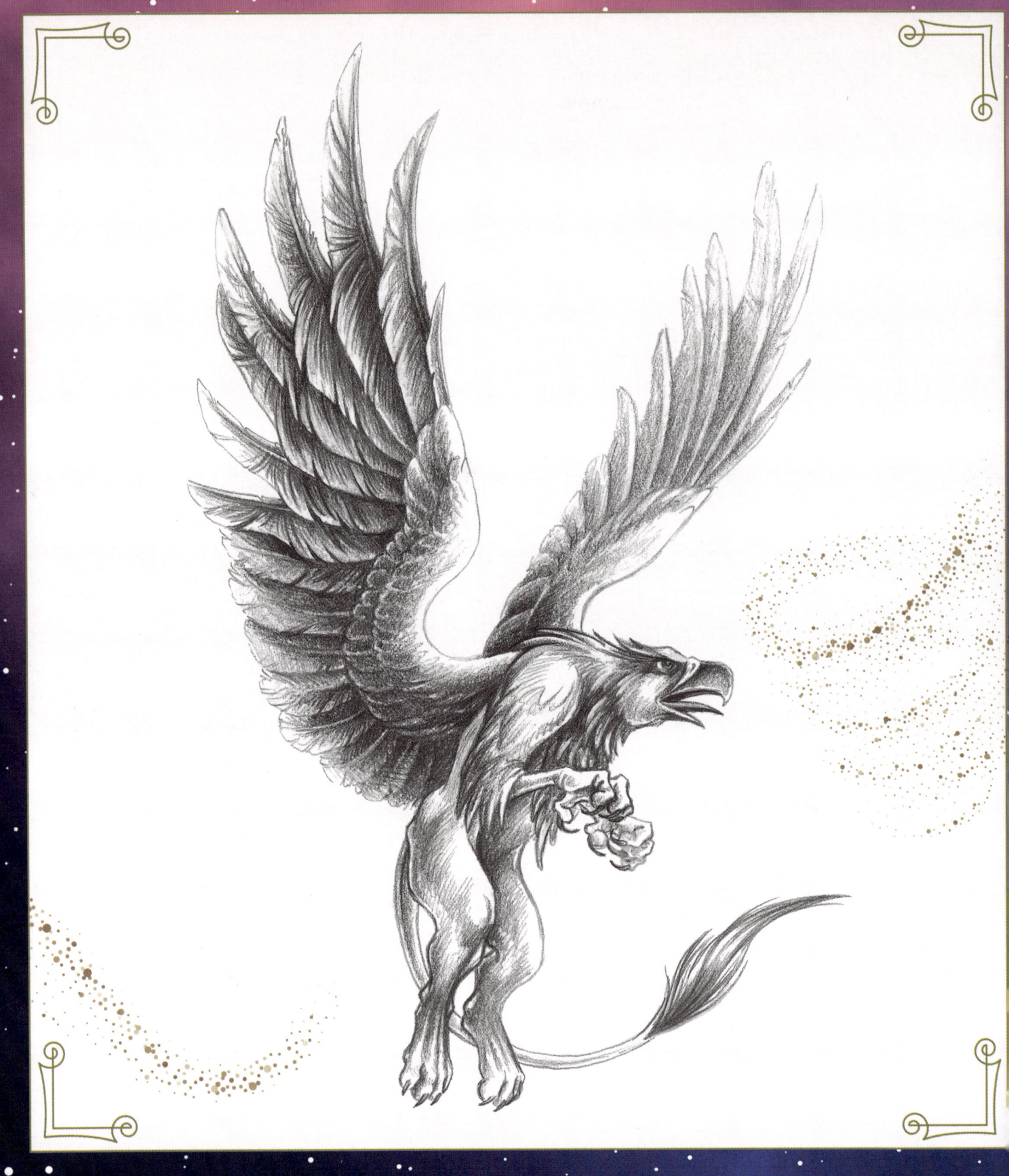

Sketch a gryphon mid-flight, wings spread wide
as its talons reach for the earth below.

Draw an ancient circle of glowing runestones,
each stone thrumming with energy.

Imagine a marketplace alive with magical wares, enchanted relics, and potions as colorful lanterns float overhead.

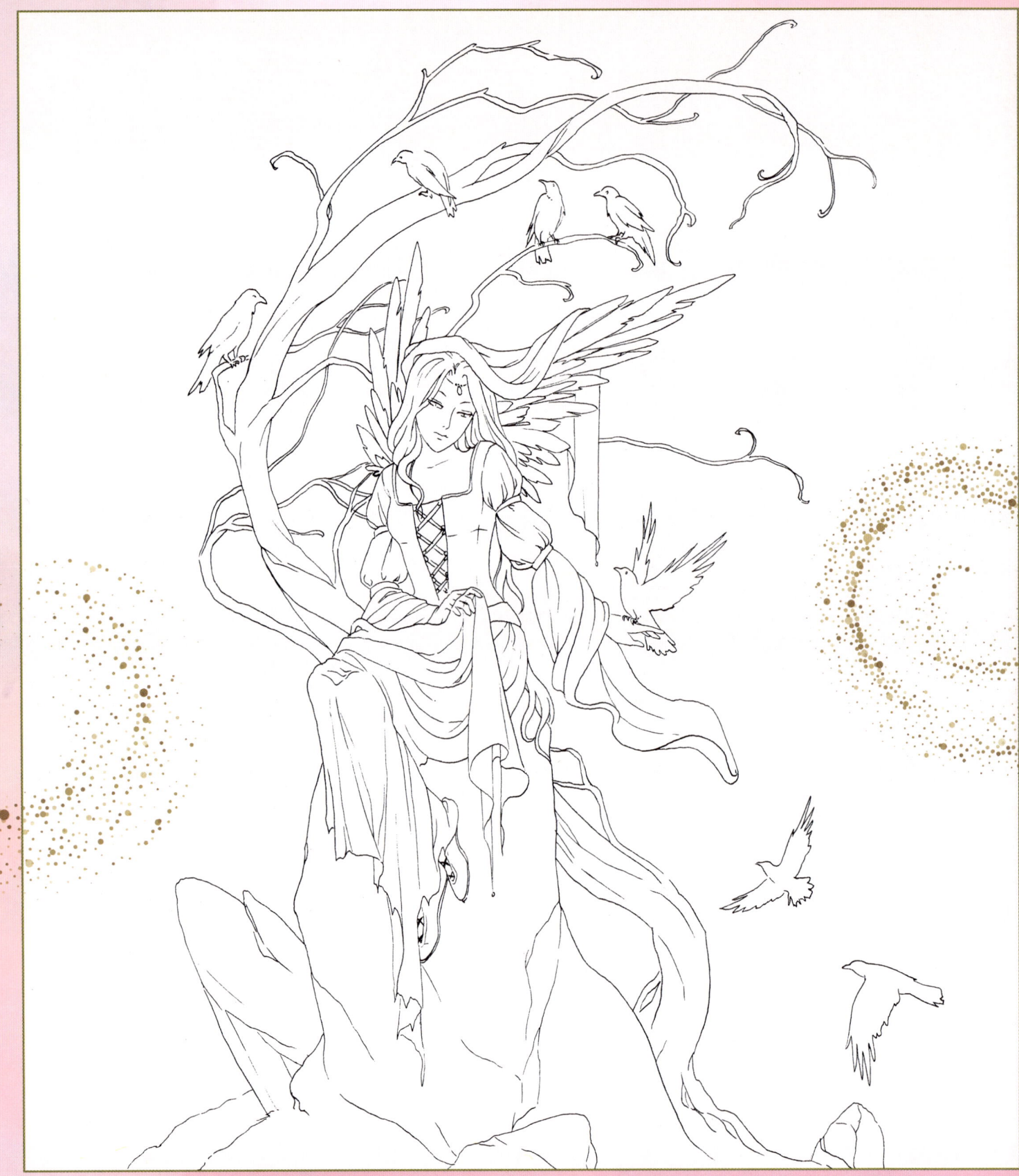

Summon a dark Celtic fae, draped in flowing robes and framed by twisted branches, her wings unfurled as birds circle her throne of stone.

Envision a midnight garden where
flowers unfurl beneath the stars,
petals glowing with secret fire.

Portray a desert of ancient bones,
sand shifting over half-buried
skeletal remains.

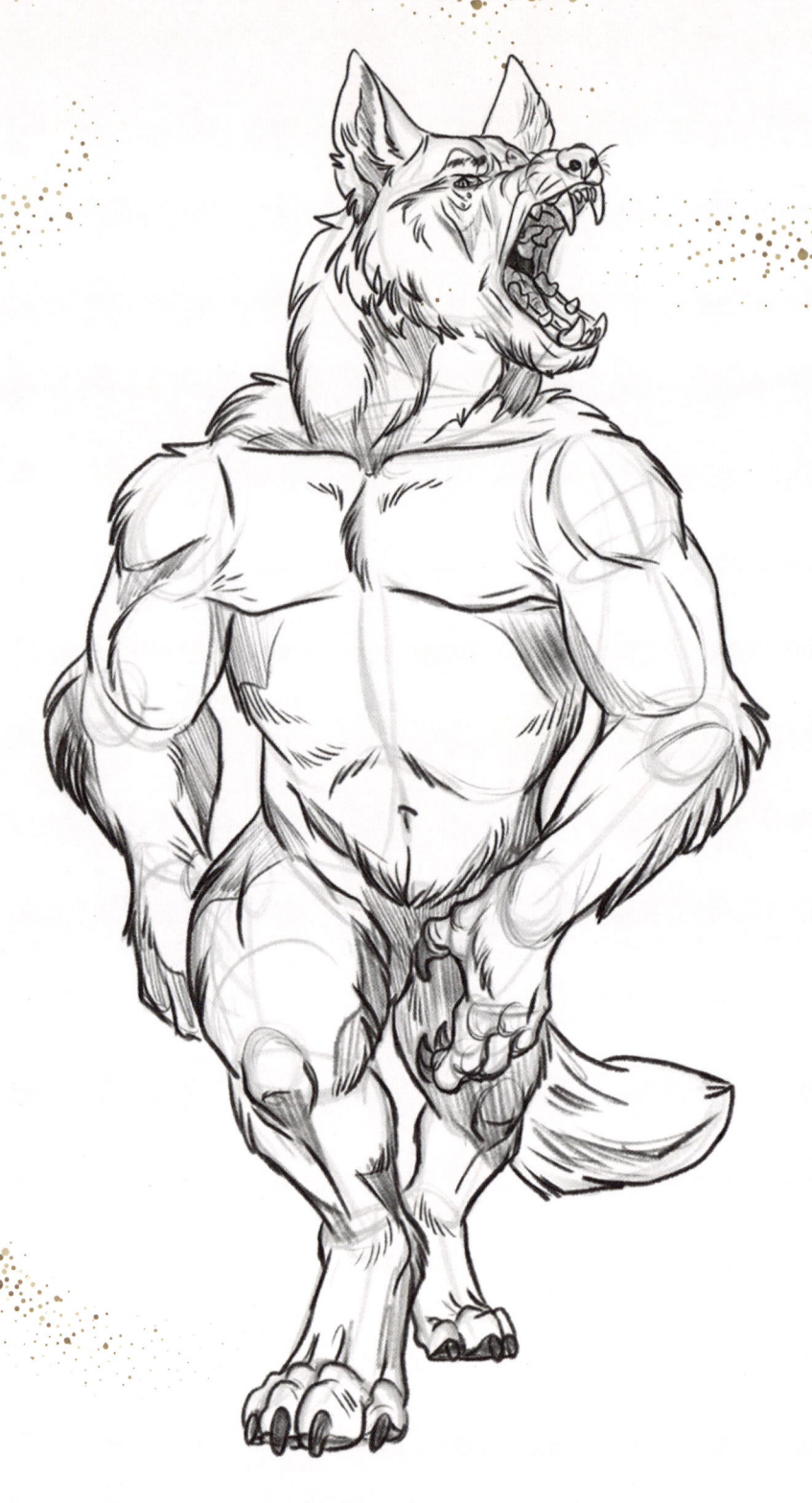

Sketch a towering werewolf mid-roar, muscles taut, and fangs bared to the night.

Envision a fortress that seems carved from night itself.

Imagine a wishing well whose waters flash with strange light.

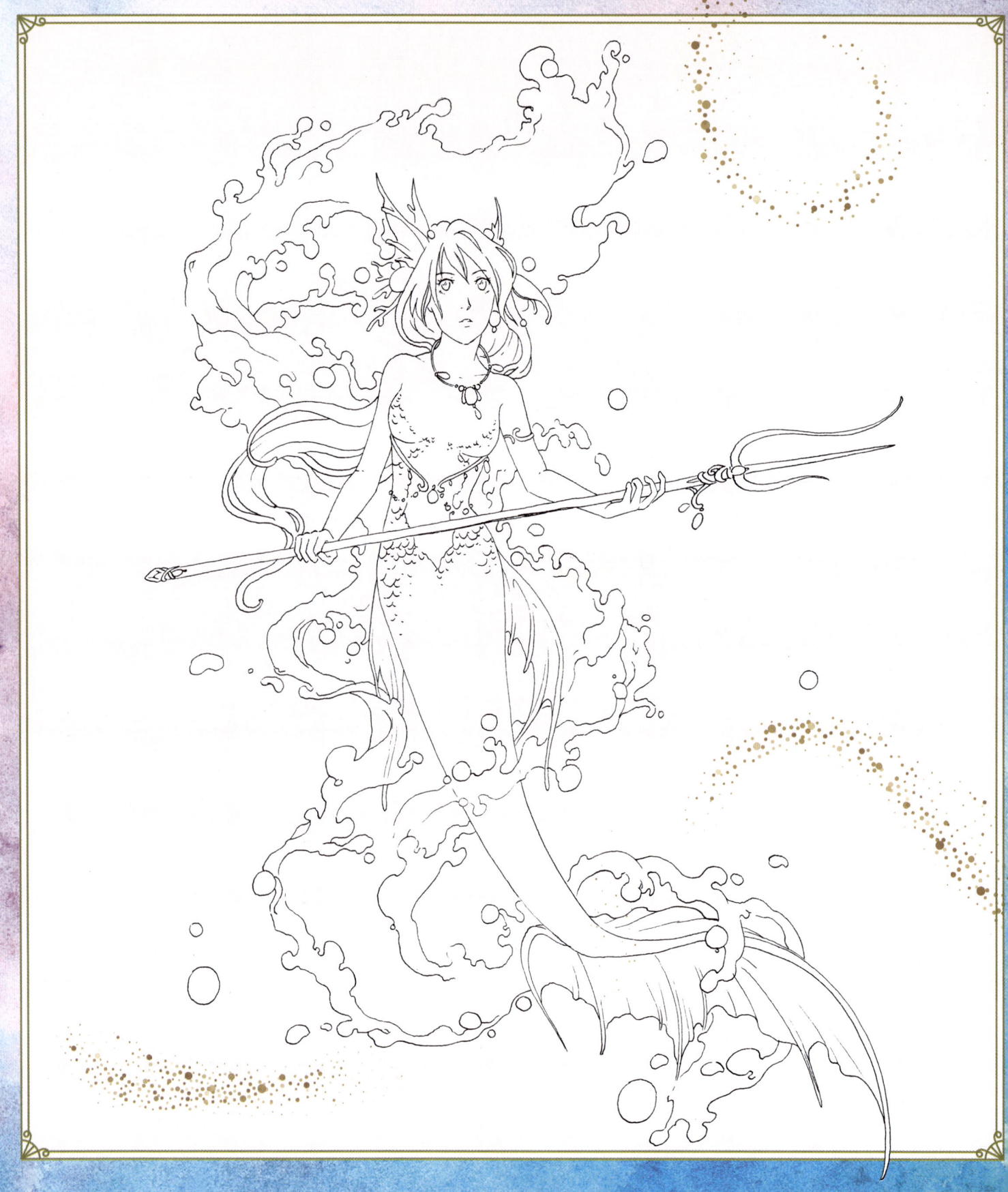

Depict a mermaid queen wielding a trident, her hair drifting like seaweed
and her tail coiled in waves that shimmer like living water.

Envision a crown wrought from starlight,
glittering with constellations.

Sketch a ship battling waves
beneath lightning-streaked skies.

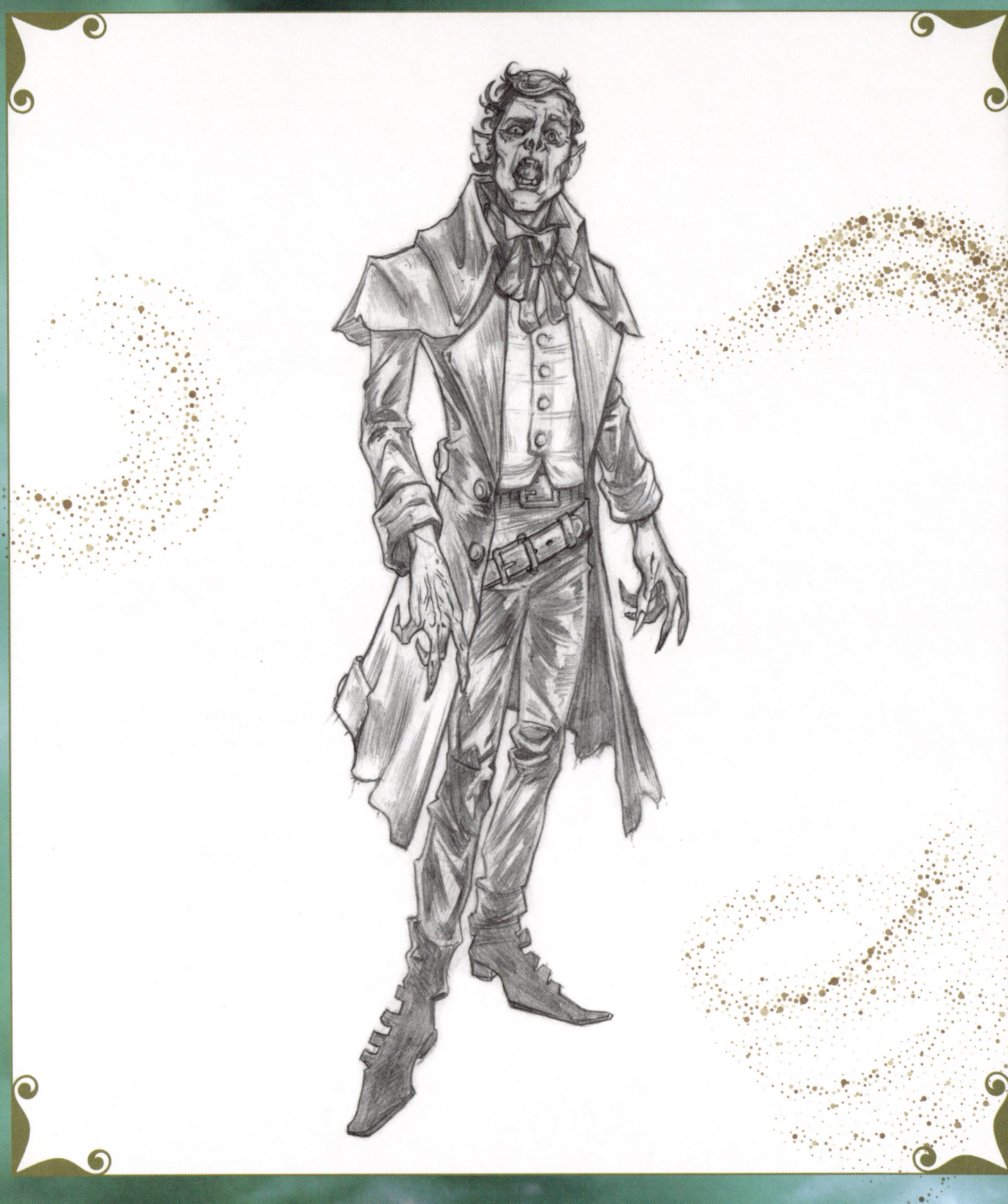

Capture a darkly romantic vampire, pale and ageless, eyes burning with secrets.

Draw a stag crowned with glowing antlers
as he glides through the shadowy mist.

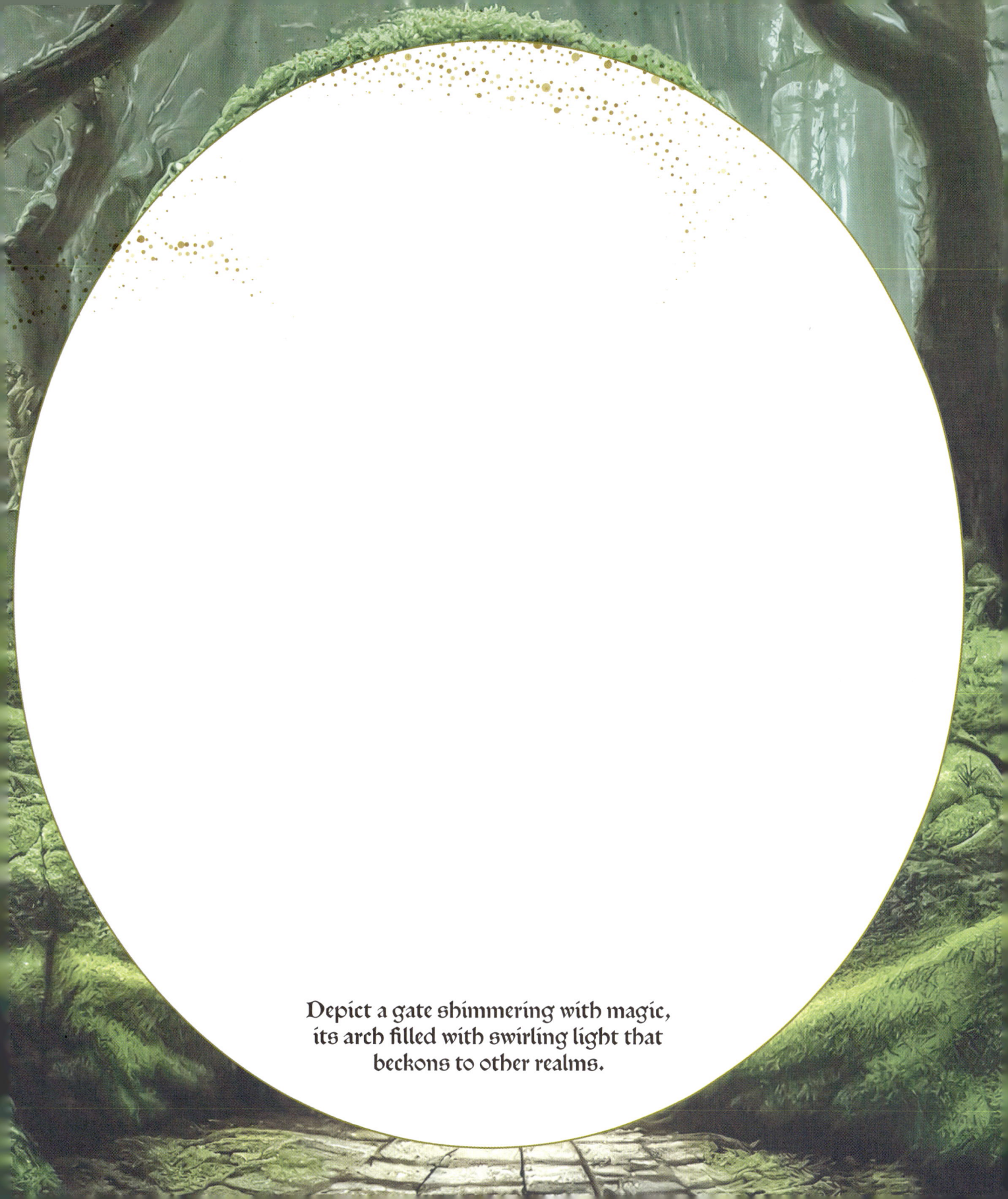

Depict a gate shimmering with magic,
its arch filled with swirling light that
beckons to other realms.

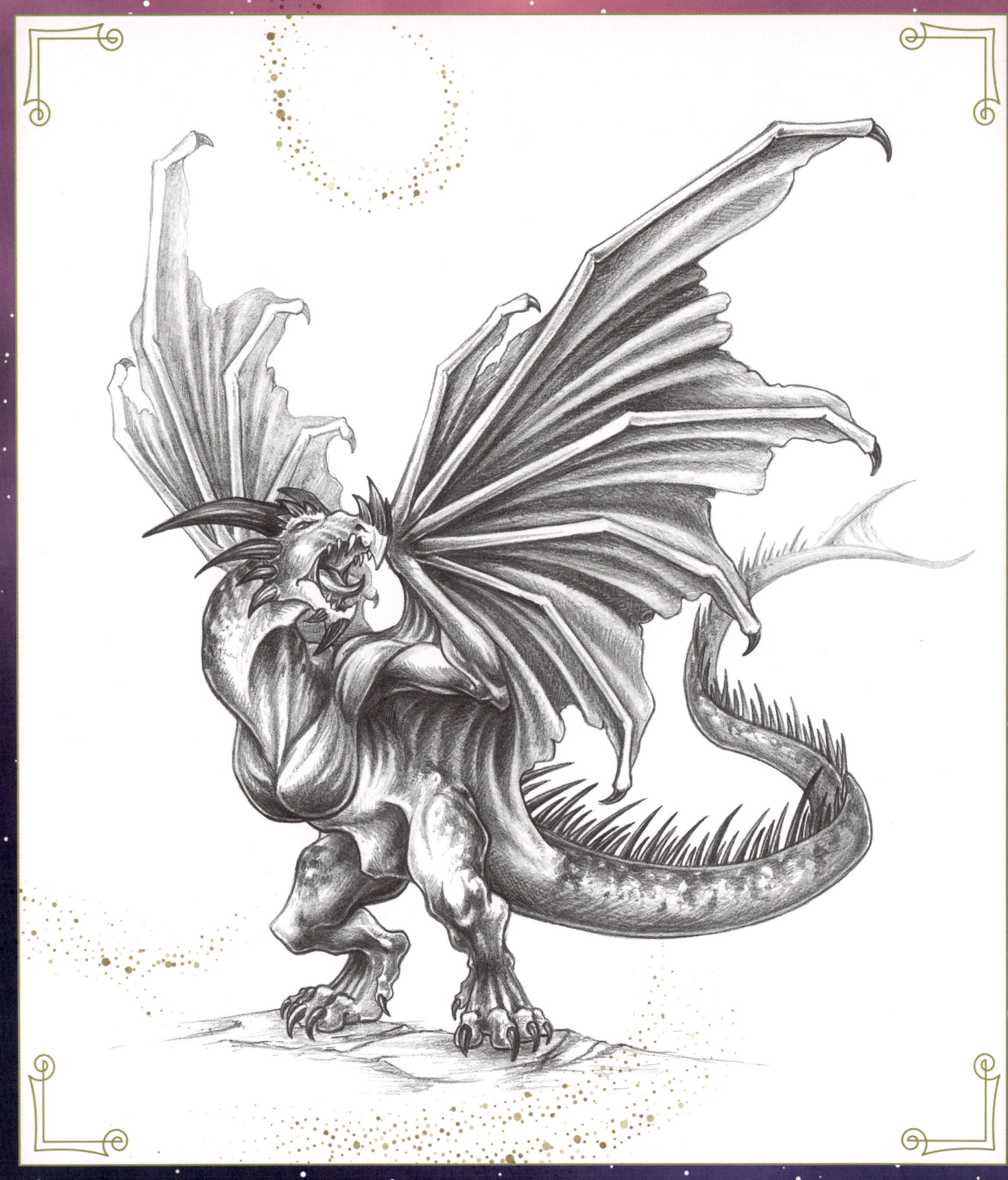

Sketch a menacing wyvern with jagged wings and a barbed tail, rearing back to strike.

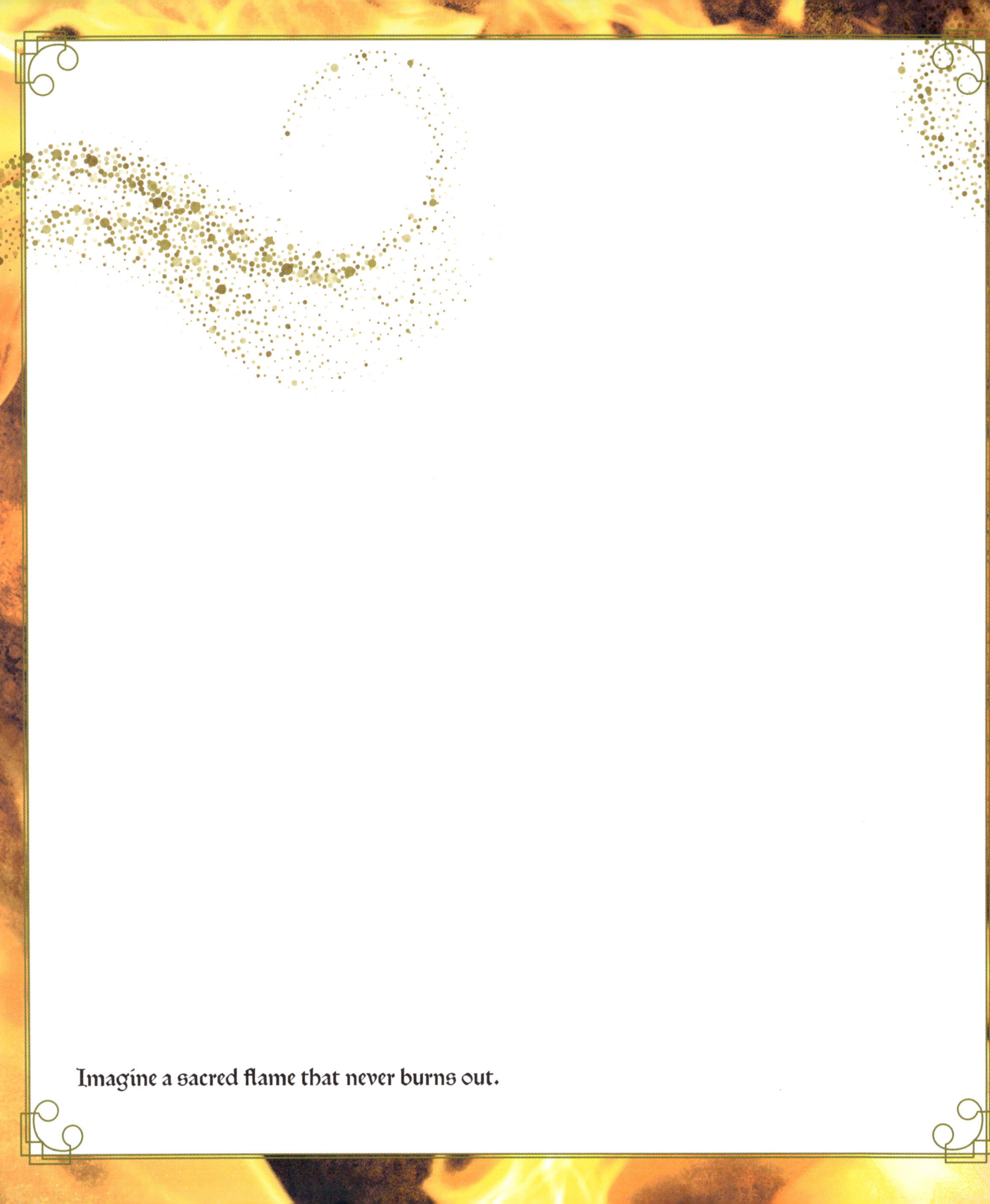

Imagine a sacred flame that never burns out.

Sketch a glass tower rising from a plain, its transparent walls shimmering like crystal.

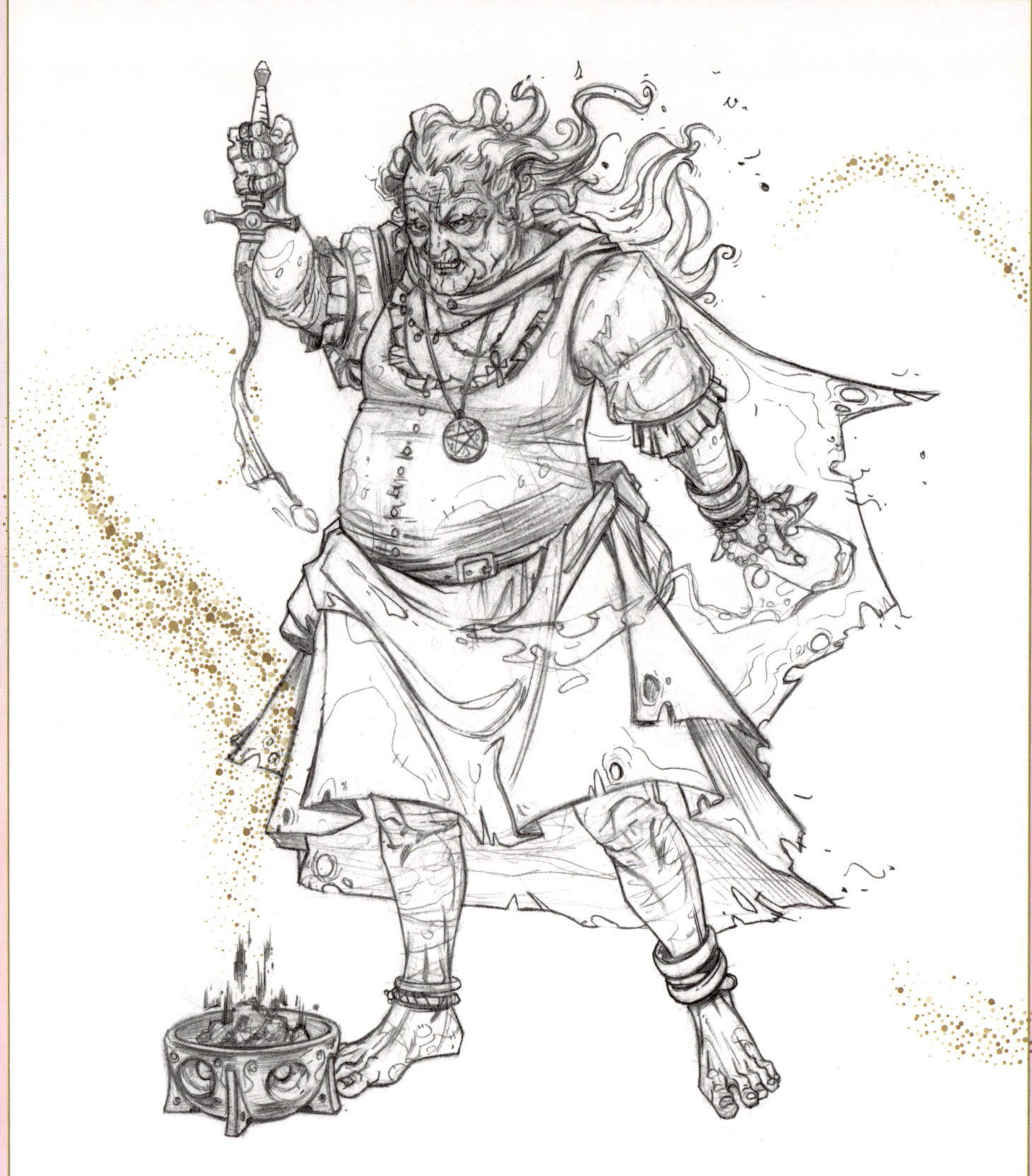

Envision a witch mid-spell, conjuring a dagger
from the smoke and flame from her cauldron.

Capture a bridge made of light spanning a deep chasm.

Depict a shattered crown lying on stone steps, its fragments scattered across the floor of an abandoned throne room.

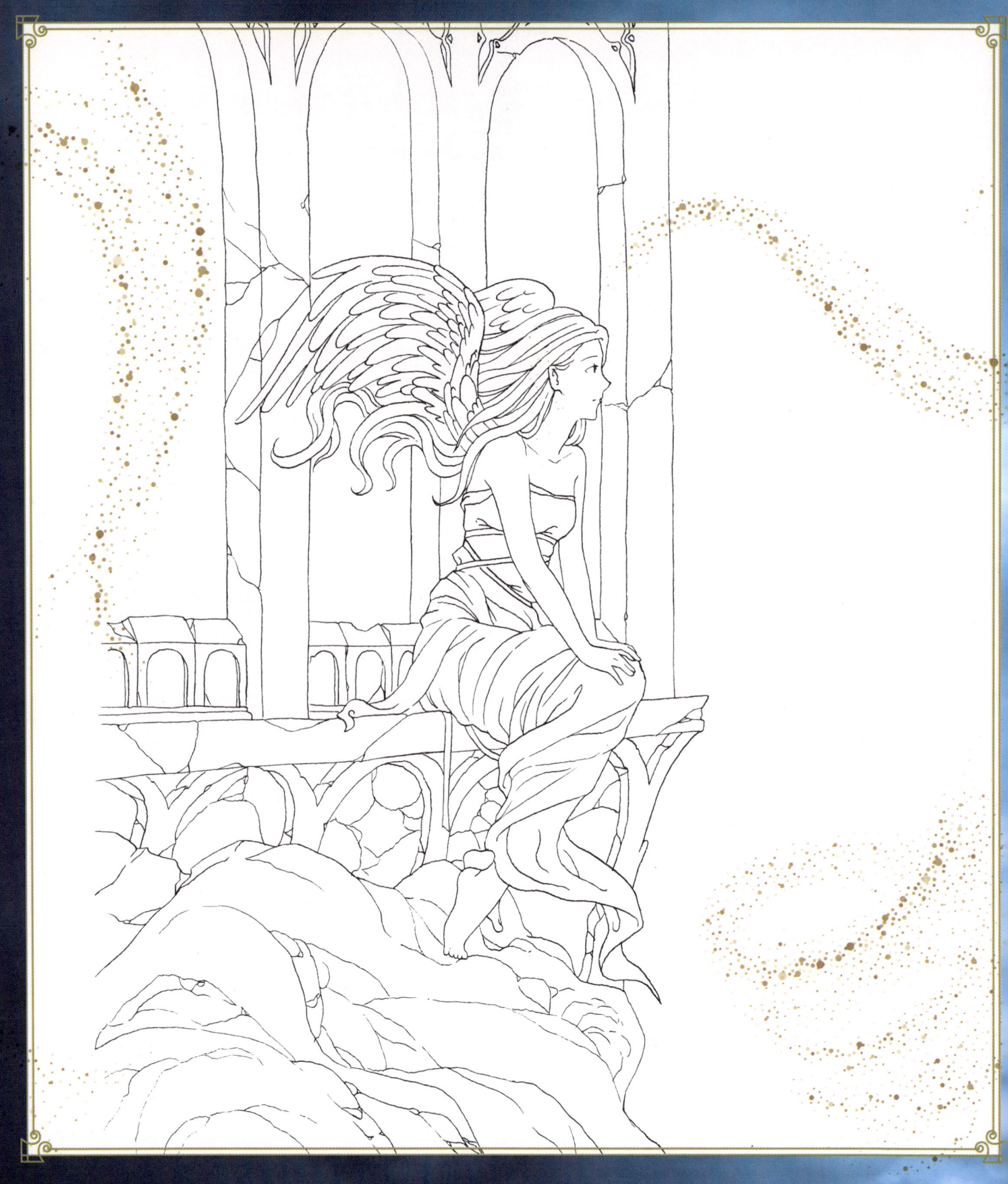

Imagine a castle adrift in the clouds, an angelic figure
perched on a high balcony, wings spread against the heavens.

Imagine a cloaked stranger striding into the mist,
face hidden yet every step heavy with destiny.

Envision a celestial waterfall, starlight pouring like liquid silver into a pool.

Quarto.com
WalterFoster.com

© 2026 Quarto Publishing

First Published in 2026
by Walter Foster Publishing,
an imprint of The Quarto Group,
100 Cummings Center, Suite 265-D,
Beverly, MA 01915, USA.
T (978) 282-9590 F (978) 283-2742

Content originally found in the following titles:

Art of Drawing Fantasy Characters
978-1-6005-8166-3
Artwork pages 2, 3, 4, 16, 28, 44, 64, 72
© 2010 by Jacob Glaser

Watercolor Made Easy: Fairies & Fantasy
978-1-6005-8141-0
Artwork 12, 20, 40, 52, 60, 78
© 2009 by Meredith Dillman

Drawing Made Easy: Dragons & Fantasy
978-1-6005-8068-0
Artwork pages 8, 32, 48, 68
© 2009 by Joana Contreras (Kythera of Anevern)

Draw Like an Artist: 100 Fantasy Creatures and Characters
978-1-6315-9964-4
Artwork pages 24, 36, 56
© 2020 by Brynn Metheney

EEA Representation, WTS Tax d.o.o.,
Žanova ulica 3, 4000 Kranj, Slovenia.
www.wts-tax.si

Walter Foster Publishing titles are also available at discount for
retail, wholesale, promotional, and bulk purchase. For details,
contact the Special Sales Manager by email at specialsales@
quarto.com or by mail at The Quarto Group, Attn: Special Sales
Manager, 100 Cummings Center, Suite 265-D, Beverly, MA
01915, USA.

29 28 27 26 25   1 2 3 4 5

ISBN: 978-1-5771-5840-0

Design: Cindy Samargia Laun
Cover Image: Lindsay Archer

Printed in Guangdong, China TT012026